God's Best Is Me
Living To Please God

"Walk as children of light in all goodness
And truth, trying to learn what is pleasing to the Lord."

Ephesians 5:8-10

by

Dr. Jeanne Sheffield

authorHOUSE®

AuthorHouse™
1663 Liberty Drive
Bloomington, IN 47403
www.authorhouse.com
Phone: 1-800-839-8640

Published by AuthorHouse 2/4/2013

ISBN: 978-1-4817-0754-1 (sc)
ISBN: 978-1-4817-0753-4 (e)

About the Author

Dr. Jeanne Sheffield's life has taken many twists and turns, leading her to the delightful discovery of directing children and helping them transform their lives.

She started her career in show business, first as a TV performer and singer on national TV, later as a music teacher to youth. Eventually she was asked to work in the inner city of Memphis, Tennessee with at risk children. It was there that she recognized the many challenges that children and teens encounter and why secular methods fail in their approach to reach them. Over time she began to integrate the transformational teachings of the Bible in ways that were both fun, meaningful, and effective for all ages.

As a result, this twenty five topic book covering many issues facing our youth today was born; boldly based on the character of Christ-like living principles that have been proven to be enduring, enriching, and an effective means of living. Her experiences working with troubled children eventually led her to enroll and complete her Masters degree in Christian Counseling and her Doctorate in Theology from Jacksonville Theological Seminary.

Dr. Jeanne Sheffield's mission is for parents and their children to learn and appreciate the value of the application of the *God's Best Is Me* studies. She originally created this workbook as an instructor-led self-enrichment program. It works for children of various ages who need to develop essential social skills, etiquette, and character values with a methodology that will keep their attention.

Never before have our youth been in such desperate need for higher standards and moral enrichment. By using this in-depth program, Dr. Jeanne feels that the children of America will be headed in the right direction. *God's Best Is Me* is a gift she has been inspired to create for our children and teens. Her heart's desire is to help them visualize and actualize their dreams by teaching them how to aspire to become a true "quality person" emulating the character and etiquette of Christ.

Dedications

*"It's in Christ that we find out who we are and what we are living for.
Long ago, before we first heard of Christ, He had His eye on us,
Had designs on us for glorious living, part of the overall purpose
He is working out in everything and everyone."* **Ephesians 1:11**

To the Holy Spirit:
*Who whispered in my heart to teach and write this book
Who gave me thoughts and answers or showed me another way
And who is my closest companion in my journey here on earth*

To My Mother:
*Who saw through God's eyes the woman I could be
Who stays beside me through all my joys and trials
And who will always and forever be my dearest, sweetest friend
…words cannot express my love, Mama…*

To Deborah Kelly, My Editor
*Who became more than the friend I asked for
Who added her creativity, incredible skills and expertise
And who shares my excitement for transforming America's youth*

To Clarence Hampton ("Hamp"), My Director
*Who was the best director in the whole world to work with
Who told me to go home and make up an etiquette program
And who is so excited that I have published my very first book!*

**To My Pastors; Rev. Jim Rowland, Dr. Steven Nielsen, Dr. Ray Self,
Rev. Don Johnson, Dr. Barbara Adams, Pastor Rick Bennett, and
Pastor Greta Hunter**
*Who have each played a big part in my growth and transformation
Who have given me words of knowledge, truth, and discernment
And who share my passion for God, His presence, His touch, His call*

To All My Friends
*Who have lent me a shoulder at times (especially Phil's) Who have never said give it up, but
said it will happen…And who I wouldn't trade for anything on earth…*
God Bless You All

Practicing Setting A Table

Studying Course Lessons *Graduation*

*** Letter to Parents ***

**"Hold the image of the life you want
and make that image become fact." -
*Norman Vincent Peale***

Thank you for choosing *God's Best Is Me* as an important part of your child's development!

This program began because of my concern as a teacher in an inner city program in Memphis for young children and teenagers. My observations deeply troubled me, because my students obviously needed more than the contemporary music classes I was teaching. They needed someone interested and concerned about addressing the important issues pertaining to their development; issues such as self-esteem, character values, and common courtesy. The youth of America are exposed to a very harsh, self-serving and rude world – a world that has lost many of the values that our grandparents taught us in years gone by. It is with JOY that I have created this special program that will educate and inspire our youth to recapture those values and apply them to their lives today.

As creator and author of *God's Best Is Me*, it is my heart's desire and mission to offer our youth the most inspiring, pivotal program parents could ever find to teach them to become quality people. Young people must be inspired and challenged to reach higher, to 'visualize and realize' their dreams, believing that there is a special purpose for their lives. This kind of encouragement can bring about a delightful transformation to even the most difficult child. Each child who studies *God's Best Is Me* will be opened up to a healthy self-image because of its dynamic creative and motivational studies. This weekly 'jam-packed' study is filled with contagious enthusiasm and topics intended to grab your child's attention and put to immediate use these valuable skills.

I look forward to hearing what you and your child have to say when your child has completed *God's Best Is Me*.

Sincerely,

Jeanne Sheffield, Th.D

God's Best Is Me

Student Manual

Hello and welcome to *God's Best Is Me*! My name is Dr. Jeanne Sheffield and I am so thrilled and excited for YOU! You have decided to choose *God's Best Is Me* to be your study guide in two very important areas in your life – your Character Development and the practice of good Etiquette!

My goal as author of *God's Best Is Me* is to inspire you to become a person of integrity and a person with confidence, poise, and grace in all situations. When you learn to integrate these wonderful values you will develop the attributes of a genuine "quality person", a person complete and happy within. We are living in a world that often pairs us with rude, self-serving people, those who have forgotten good manners and even common courtesy. It can really be hard to remember our own good manners and courtesy when faced with such mean behavior! Have you asked yourself, "What can I do to make things better?" The answer begins with <u>You</u>. It begins with the choices you make each day. Your life touches so many people. What you say and how you live your life make a big impact on others. God gives us the freedom to choose each day what we will do with our lives. I'm so glad you have chosen to spend quality time learning with *God's Best Is Me*. My desire is that what you learn here will be one of the more rewarding experiences of your life.

But before we go any further, let's look at the meaning of the word grace and you will understand why I chose the title of this special study to be *God's Best Is Me*. *Grace* means to have favor: the favor of God, not for anything we have done or will ever do, but because God loves us unconditionally. *Grace* means to have beauty. It means to have a beautiful spirit within. It also means to possess charm, poise, and expression.

While planning this study for you, I could not think of anyone more suited than the Apostle Paul to be your mentor and teacher. Paul, as you may already know, lived his life as a devoted Christian who wrote over half of the New Testament. Paul was also a great and inspiring teacher of the word of God and was held in high esteem for his character and integrity. Now do you see why I chose the name *God's Best Is Me?* It is the Apostle Paul that we will want to emulate as he teaches us to walk in the footsteps and grace of Jesus Christ. We will be following Paul's guidelines to becoming a true quality person as we grow in our character studies. We will also have a great time studying proper etiquette and creating good habits as we leave the old ones behind.

You are going to experience these *graceful attributes* for the next several weeks when you study your *God's Best Is Me* chapters covering such topics as "Cool Manners Make Big Impressions" and "Checking My Character Within." You will begin to see a noticeable change in how you view your life and those around you. I know you will be excited to share with others how to be a kinder, gentler, and more thoughtful person.

We can transform our lives and the world around us with thoughts, words, and actions. Let's do it together! You may want to tell your friends about *God's Best Is Me* as well!

Let's take a close look at all the topics we are going to study. This is going to be a really great time to Learn, Play, Think, and Create!

Are you ready?

Let's Begin!

-The Fruits of the Spirit-

*Love, Joy, Peace Patience, Kindness, Goodness
Gentleness, Self-Control*

The Apostle's Pledge
"I Pledge Allegiance to You, Lord Jesus,
I will walk in Your Grace and Peace.
Create in me Your Temple, Lord, where You
will want to be.
Make my life Your Vessel
Fill me with Your Living Word
So I can go and share Your Love
With those who haven't heard."

Acts of Grace

The Apostle Paul very often addressed his letters to his brothers and sisters in Christ by saying, *"Grace be unto you, my friends, and peace from God our Father."* Paul loved Jesus with all his heart and he wanted all new Christians to behave appropriately and to follow the grace of Jesus. Whether we lived in Jerusalem 2,000 years ago walking with Jesus and Paul or whether we are living today in the 21st century, grace is still "in." Walking in *grace* means to be aware, in tune with those around us. It means to be considerate and thoughtful. *Grace* means that you care.

Remember the Four Grace Words:
Thank You
Please
You're Welcome

Table of Contents

Week Three
Fruit of the Spirit: Peace

Week Four
Fruit of the Spirit: Patience

Week Five
Fruit of the Spirit: Kindness

Week Six
Fruit of the Spirit: Goodness

Elective Topics

God's Best Is Me: Songs of Praise To Live and Love By!

A Special Fruit Each Week to Carry in my Heart

Week One: *Love*
Jesus Replied: *"Love the Lord your God with all your heart and will all your soul and with all your mind." This is the first and greatest commandment. And the second is like it: "Love your neighbor as yourself." **Matthew 22:37-39***

Week Two: *Joy*
*"A cheerful look brings joy to the heart. And good news gives health to the bones." **Proverbs 15:30***

Week Three: *Peace*
*"Peace I leave with you; My Peace I give you. I do not give to you as the world gives. Do not let your hearts be troubled and do not be afraid." **John 14:27***

Week Four: *Patience*
*"Everyone should be quick to listen, slow to speak and slow to become angry." **James 1:19***

Week Five: *Kindness*
*"Pleasant words are a honeycomb sweet to the soul and healing to the bones." **Proverbs 16:24***

Week Six: *Goodness*
*"Let your light shine before men that they may see your good deeds and praise your Father in Heaven."**Matthew 5:16***

Fruits to Chew: *Faithfulness*
*"Well done my good and faithful servant! You have been faithful with a few things; I will put you in charge of many things. Come and share your Master's happiness!" **Matthew 25:21***

Gentleness
*"Be completely humble and gentle; be patient, bearing with one another in love." **Ephesians 4:2***

Self-Control
*"God did not give us a spirit of timidity, but a spirit of power, of love, and of self discipline." **2 Timothy 1:7***

Week One
Fruit of the Spirit:
Love

Love
Stretches
Your
Heart
And
Makes
You
Big

Inside

S......T......R......E......T......C......H

Week One

Begin the Day with Prayer

This Apostle's Pledge:
"I Pledge Allegiance to You, Lord Jesus, I will walk in Your Grace and Peace. Create in me Your Temple, Lord, where You Will want to be. Make my life Your Vessel Fill me with Your Living Word So I can go and share Your Love With those who haven't heard."

Acts of Grace: Thank You, Please, You're Welcome, Excuse Me

Fruit for the Week: *Love*

Practical Love Exercises

Sing Songs of Praise

Topics:

> *My Appearance*
> *The Mirror, My Friend*
> *Eye to Eye Contact*
> *Hello and Good bye*
> *Introductions*
> *Conversational Skills*
> *Being a Good Friend*

Fruit for Memory:

> *"Love the Lord with all your heart and with all your soul and with all your mind. This is the first and greatest command. And the second is like it. Love your neighbor as your self."*
> *Matthew 27:37-39*

My Appearance

Why I Should be Modest

The way we groom ourselves says much about the way we value ourselves. Our appearance plays a big part in how we walk, how we talk, how we relate to others with shyness, awkwardness or with self- confidence. It can also make us feel embarrassed or it can make us feel like a million dollars!

Our appearance does not go unnoticed. People pay attention to our hair, our posture, our clothes, the colors we wear, even the way we smell, as well as the things mentioned above. When we are out shopping, we need to use good judgment while selecting our wardrobes. We should always remember to want people to be drawn to the person we are inside and not our clothes.

Dressing modestly means that you dress in style, but you choose to be more conservative than revealing with your wardrobe. Let's look at some inappropriate ways of dressing and how we can make *modest* changes, yet still be in style.

For Girls: *The Issue is to be Feminine*

*Halter tops and other skimpy clothing
(How can we make changes here?)
*Length of dresses and skirts
(Does the length matter?)
*Multiple ear or body piercing, tattoos
(Will you want these things later in life when fads have changed and you are an adult?)
*Makeup
(When should you begin wearing it? How much should you wear?)

It is important to remember that boys are visual by nature. As young teenagers, they begin to look at girls differently. It is natural, but it is your job to dress modestly. By doing so, you will help them to practice self-control, one of the fruits of the spirit.

For Boys: *The Issue is to be Masculine*

Let's look at some inappropriate ways of dressing and see ways that will show how you, too, can be a cool and modest dresser!

*Saggy, sloppy, or grunge clothing
(How do you feel about this attire?)
*Tee shirts with inappropriate messages
(What are you telling the world? Do tee shirt messages matter?)
*Clothing with holes in it, especially in inappropriate places
(Discuss your feelings regarding this fashion statement)

Think about this…what kind of image does the way you dress communicate? What do teachers in school think when you dress immodestly? Do you think it gives them a wrong impression? Will they believe you are a good learner and student? Dressing sloppy is understandable at times in the right places. We should know there are places that require a dress code and dress accordingly. Examples include churches, schools, parties, theaters, weddings, and funerals.

Here's a fun discussion…let's see what we learn!

Girls tell the boys how they look to them and what they want them to wear. Boys tell the girls how they look to them and what they want them to wear.

We all want to have an attractive appearance. It is not important to have the most expensive clothes or even the most stylish clothes. It is having clean clothes and how we feel when we wear them. The main issue is the message that we are portraying to the world. Most importantly, we want people to look into our eyes and to notice the person inside of us! Dress modestly and carry yourself with dignity. Be proud of who you are!

Tips to Start the Day:
*A nice, clean face
*Nails, clean and filed
*Clothes neat, ironed, and clean
*Stand with good posture
Now you're set to take on the day!

The Mirror, My Friend

Checking My Character Within

Let's have some fun! Let's look at ourselves in a full-length mirror and see how we look to ourselves and to others. What do your facial expressions say? Do you look happy? Do you look sad? Do you look bored? What do you think others see when they look at you?

When you look in the mirror you should see a pleasant and well-groomed person, someone everyone will want to meet. Stand up tall. Be proud of who you are!

Let's look right into the mirror and say, *"hello you wonderful you!"*
That should make you smile and probably giggle!

"Cool Manners"
Make
"Big Impressions"

A sure way to make a good impression when you meet some someone is to show that you are cool and confident. Here is the way to do it:

Eye to Eye Contact

*First….Look them in the eye. Eye contact is extremely important. Let's discuss why. If you look to the ground, avoiding looking straight into someone's eyes, what are you saying? If you look directly into their eyes and pay attention to what they are saying, what message are you sending?

*Second…Speak clearly and be confident when you say your name. Why is this important?

*Third…Shake hands in an appropriate manner.
    (We'll discuss handshakes a little later.)

Saying Hello and Goodbye

How does greeting someone make them feel? Is it important to say hello? What do you think? Is it important to say goodbye when you are leaving?

Let's create some examples of saying *hello and goodbye*, and see whether or not it is important to us and the other person.

Example 1

Shana is walking down the hall between classes and sees her good friend Michelle.

She says, "Hi Michelle, what's up? Are we going to the movies tomorrow night?"

Michelle does not answer. She does not mean to be rude, but she is thinking about an important math test that is coming up and not paying attention. She walks right past Shana without acknowledging her.

How do you think Shana feels? Let's discuss it.

Example 2

Mark and John are supposed to play in a soccer game this afternoon and Mark is just back to school from having a bad cold.

John: "Hello, Mark! How's it going?"

Mark": "Oh, hi John!"

John: "Are you up to the game today? I heard it's gonna be tough!"

Mark: "Sure, I'm fine now, I just had a cold. I'm ready!"

John: "Great, I'll see you at 3:30. Goodbye!"

Mark: "Goodbye!"

What did their greetings say about their relationship? What did their "good-byes" say? It is so important to bring closure when we greet people and when we leave them, because it makes you both feel valued and important. How does it make you feel?

Remember to always say "hello" and "goodbye"!

Your Handshake

A firm handshake says a lot about your self-confidence. Never give a limp handshake, not even to a girl or woman! We call this kind of handshake a "limp fish". Also, never *squeeze* someone's hand. We call this painful kind of grip the "bone crusher". Remember that people wear rings, especially females, and you must not get carried away with a crushing handshake!

A good handshake is gentle, brief, and firm. Be careful not to "pump" the other person's arm!

Let's practice shaking hands with each other so we can get a feel for different sized hands and evaluate each other's grip. Do not stand too close to the other person; you should stand an arm's length away.

Conversational Skills

Let's pretend you just met someone you have never met before. How should you start the conversation? Maybe you could start by asking a question:

"Where do you go to school?"
    "What grade are you in?"
"Do you play soccer/basketball/football?"
    "What CD's do you have?"
"Who's your favorite band?"

Never ask personal questions. They are always inappropriate.
Examples of inappropriate questions are:

"You dad is never around when I come over. Are your parents divorced or is he out of town a lot?"
    "Those are cool shoes. How much did they cost?"
"Why is your mom's last name Mitchell and your last is Johnson?"
    "You don't look like the rest of your sisters. Are you adopted?"
Another example of an inappropriate question would be asking an adult how hold she or he is.

Respect another person's privacy, no matter how curious you may be!

Introductions

<u>Example 1</u>

Introducing a friend to a teacher:

You will address the teacher first, with respect.
"Mrs. Owens, I'd like you to meet my new friend, Allison.
Allison, this is my teacher, Mrs. Owens."

Allison: "Hello, Mrs. Owens, I have heard so much about you!"

Mrs. Owens: "Well thank you, Allison! Welcome to my class!"

Allison: "Thank you. I'm excited to be here!"

<u>Example 2</u>

Introducing a friend to two old friends.

"Linda and Gary, I'd like you to meet Michael."
Linda and Gary hold out their hands to shake hands with Michael.

Gary: "Nice to meet you! Is it "Michael" or "Mike"?

Mike: "Well, I really like to be called 'Mike'. Nice to meet you guys, too.!"

How to be a Good Friend

Creating the Spirit of Friendship

Let's discuss what you think would be a good definition of a friend. You may have heard the old saying, *"a friend is someone who really knows you...and likes you anyway!"* A friend is someone who comes when every else goes. With a true friend, you do not have to be on your very best behavior all the time. You can just be yourself!

Psychologists tell us that one of the main problems in America today is loneliness... we all need a friend! In Genesis 2, God created the world and He saw that Adam was lonely, so what did He do? He created a friend and "helpmate" for Adam named Eve.

A friendship can be a spirit between people. Have you heard coaches talk about team spirit before a game? What do you think they mean? Team spirit means thinking alike, playing alike, and putting your hearts into the game. When two or more people are united with the same kind of friendship, their relationship takes on a special light. From that light, friends help each other, share with each other, and support each other.

Is loyalty important in a friendship? Don't you want your friend to be someone you can count on during the happy times *and* the sad times? Do you want someone who will tell you the truth, even if it hurts to hear it?

Who will you tell your secrets? Should you test your friend? A true friend should have integrity and will be loyal to your friendship.

Friends and the spirit of friendship are not a matter of chance; they are a matter of choice. Why do friends depend on us more than they depend on others?

What Qualities Should You Look for in a Friend?

- A person who is non-judgmental and accepts you the way you are

- A person who likes the same things you do

- A person who knows how to compromise and play fair

- A person who likes who she or he is and is fun to be around

Make friendships a priority in life.

Consider how your choices and decisions will affect them. Remember that friendships die just like flowers when they are not given attention. Never take a good friend for granted…faithful friends are hard to find!

Be a giver.

Be kind without expecting kindness. Be loving without expecting to be loved in return.

Be appreciative.

Take time to let your friends know how much they mean to you. Find ways to express your thanks. Find a little happy gift and add a card with a special note only the two of you would understand. Friends always like to know how much you value them!

Remember that friends are very special gifts to treasure. Some friendships will last a lifetime if you take special care of them!

Because friendship is so important, I would like you to take the time to write about a special friend in your life. Tell why your friend is important to you, how long you have been friends, why you are friends, and what your friendship means to both of you.

If you have had an unpleasant experience with a friendship, you may write about why this friendship was disappointing. Tell what you have learned from this experience. (*author's note: If papers are written in a group setting, you may instruct the students that they do not have to reveal anything too personal about their friends. The students may also want to vote on the most interesting paper.)

Character Traits of Friendship

- *"Be slow at choosing a friend and slow at losing one."* --Benjamin Franklin

- What do good friends do? They stick with you!

- A good friend is worth more than a thousand acquaintances.

- A good friend must be kind. What is kindness? Moral goodness toward one another.

- A good friend loves at all times.

- Good friends are trustworthy and stay committed. When those around us seem empty of kindness, we must reach out in love!

- A good friend possesses all the fruits of the spirit. Please turn in your Bible and read Galatians 5:22-23.

- A good friend must be honest and straight up with you. Turn to Proverbs 27:5-6 and read what the scripture says.

- A good friend is always loyal.

God is for YOU. He is always by your side and He is your *best* friend. He has all the attributes and more of a good and loyal friend. God wants a real, loving relationship with you. He wants a "closer than close" friendship with you. Do you want that with Him? If so, tell Him and spend some real "quality time" with Him. You will be surprised at what a precious friendship will develop for the two of you!

Can friendships be disappointing? Have you ever had a friend disappoint you? Have you ever disappointed or hurt a friend? Do you think you should test a potential friend before claiming them as a friend? We have talked a lot about being a friend. Let's create two different scenes that will give us a clear picture of what to look for and what *not* to look for in a friend.

Exercise 1: A Disappointing Friend

Debbie has wanted to be a cheerleader since she was a little girl. She has been practicing her routines for several weeks. Today was her big chance to get to finally see her dream come true! She auditioned with a group of girls from school for the team's coach and gave it her all. She came home feeling like she really might have a chance to win and she is anxiously waiting for a phone call with the news.

(the phone rings & Debbie jumps to answer it)

Debbie: "Hello!"

Felicia: "Hi Deb!"

Debbie: "Oh, hi Felicia! I thought you might be the coach calling!"

Felicia: "No, it's just me. I just wanted to tell you that I thought you really did great at the audition!"

Debbie: "Oh thanks, I really worked hard to learn the routines."

Felicia: "But you wouldn't believe what Lana and Kerrie were saying. They think that you shouldn't get on the team because they'll have to spend too much time teaching you all the old routines. They also said you should lose some weight!"

Debbie: "You know, Felicia, I really don't need to hear all that kind of talk. I gave my very best today, so if you're really my friend, you would not need to tell me thinks to hurt me."

Felicia: "Well, I'm sorry! I thought you might want to know what you're up against!"

Debbie: "Excuse me, but I have another call coming in."

What do you think about Felicia? Is she a friend you can trust? What could Felicia have said to build Debbie up instead of bringing her down? Is she sensitive to Debbie's feelings? Why did she tell her what the other girls said about her weight? Is there some jealousy here with Felicia? Friendship is about encouraging each other. When you think of this scenario, do you think a friend should be tested? Should a friend stand up for you when others say unkind things about you? It's really something to think about. What do you think about what Debbie told Felicia? Let's discuss it.

Exercise 2: Being a Good Friend

Being a good friend and having a good friend requires responsibility. Let's look back at some of the attributes of *both sides to friendship* and review our list. Why don't we take a few minutes to see what our role players have to teach us about *friendship*, one of the most important roles of life:

Phil and Jeanie have been friends since they first met at band practice. When Jeanie dropped her brand new clarinet and chipped her mouth piece she cried out,

Jeanie: "Oh no! My mom saved every dime just so I could have this! What am I going to do? How can I fix it?"

Phil, as usual, came to her rescue when he saw her drop it.

Phil: "Don't worry Jeanie, you can have mine for now until you can get another one. I have an extra one in my case. I guess it was waiting there just for you!"

Jeanie gives Phil a big hug!

Jeanie: "I should have known, you always seem to be there when I need you, Phil. I know I can always count on you."

Phil: "You got that right, Jeanie-Beanie, I'm always here for you!"

Jeanie & Phil: *"That's What Friends Are For."*

Throughout life, we will play many roles: mother, father, sister, brother, teacher, doctor, coach, lawyer, the list goes on and on. But the role of a good friend is very special, because a good friend will last a lifetime when other roles may change.

Having someone share your deepest secrets and dreams, and having someone support you and encourage you when times are hard is what we all need. This is a good friend and they are not easy to find. So when you test a potential friend who you feel is worthy of your loyalty and trust (and they of yours), you can consider yourself a very lucky person. Treasure your friends and they will treasure you!

How Can We Correct a Friend through Love?

- Correct them gently. Build them up, not down.

- Approach them when they are not feeling sad or upset.

- Never correct a person unless you are willing to be corrected.

- Be helpful and constructive.

- Friends shape friends. (Who is shaping you? Be selective and careful with whom you spend your time.)

- Cheer each other on! Stop being jealous of another's happiness or prosperity. Wish the very best for your friend and watch how happiness and prosperity will come to you!

- Remember to take care of your friends and they will remember to do the same for you.

- God is your very best friend. He loves you more than anyone and He is on call 24/7!

Share this special poem with a good friend:

My Real Good Friend

Are you my real good friend?
Would you say I can count on you?

Are you my real good friend?
Are you loyal, honest and truly true?

'Cause if you are, then I have a found a treasure.
Yeah, if you are, then I'm the lucky one.

'Cause if you are, we'll be close friends forever.
Sharin' the good times,
Carin' through the hard times.

Lovin' life because we've found a friend.

Are you my real good friend?
One to tell my secrets to?

Are you my real good friend?
Can you make me smile when I'm feelin' blue?

'Cause if you are, then I've found a treasure.
Yeah, if you are, something tells me
I won't ever have to wonder

Something tells me

I'm the luckiest one.

By Jeanne Sheffield

Weekly Lesson Review

Love

Let's review what we have learned! Fill in on the lines below your answers to the following questions for this week's *Fruit of the Spirit* so you can see to use this in your daily activities.

What you have learned about this week's Fruit of the Spirit?

List the important character values that you have learned from this week's fruit.

a.

b

c.

d.

e.

Describe five skills that you will use to demonstrate your knowledge of this week's fruit.

a.

b.

c.

d.

e.

___

(Hints: How do you show your love? When do you give your love? What do you say when someone says thank you for helping me? Where do you look when someone is talking to you?)

God gives us the fruits of the spirit to help us balance out the way we live.
*That includes the way we **think**, the way we **act**, and*
*the way we **treat others** and **ourselves**.*

It also means that when we "chew on the fruits" every day we are living our lives like Jesus!

This week
I want to give my
Love
by:

Praying to God

Singing Songs of Love

Reading the Bible

Memorizing my weekly scripture in my heart

Going to church to learn about God's Love

Having a Loving Attitude

Being Kind and Thoughtful

Being Forgiving

Sharing the Love of Jesus

Week Two
Fruit of the Spirit: Joy

Joy
Is
Contagious

Week Two

Begin the Day with Prayer

This Apostle's Pledge:
"I Pledge Allegiance to You, Lord Jesus,
I will walk in Your Grace and Peace.
Create in me Your Temple, Lord, where You
Will want to be.
Make my life Your Vessel
Fill me with Your Living Word
So I can go and share Your Love
With those who haven't heard."

Acts of Grace: Thank You, Please, You're Welcome, Excuse Me

Fruit for the Week: *Joy*

Practicing Joy Exercises

Sing Songs of Praise

Topics:
> *Telephone Etiquette*
> *Attitude Equals Gratitude*
> *Punctuality Counts*

Fruit for Memory:
> "A cheerful look brings joy to the heart, and gives good health to the bones." Proverbs 15:30

Telephone Etiquette

The way you talk over the phone, the way you receive messages, and the way you leave a message gives us a clue about your character and who you are.

Here are some good rules to follow that will give others the idea that you are an interesting person to talk to!

1. <u>Greeting the Caller</u>: Say "hello" with a smile in your voice. Do not answer the phone with an *I don't care* attitude. Put "life" in your words.

    Example: "Hello, this is the Johnson's residence. May I help you?" Always use proper language. Do not answer "Yeah that's right, this is the Johnson's. Wait a minute."

    If the caller wants to speak to your Mom or Dad, do not explain what they are doing if Mom or Dad cannot come to the phone. Never tell a caller anything personal that your family may be doing. Tell the caller that she or he is unavailable and ask if you can take a message.

2. <u>Being Prepared for a Call</u>: Always have a pencil and paper near the phone to take messages so that you do not have to leave your caller hanging on the phone. Write the name, phone number, time of call, and any important information. Remember to say goodbye when you finish the call.

    Let's pretend we have an answering machine and we will leave a brief out-going message. Speak slowly and clearly. Say goodbye.

3. <u>Answering Machine Out-Going Message</u>: "Thank you for calling the Woodson's. We are not available to take your call. Please leave a message and your phone number. We will call you as soon as possible. Have a great day! Goodbye."

    Create your own message on a piece of paper using the above example as your guide. Read your messages to each other. Which messages have a "smile" in them? Which messages are the clearest?

4. <u>Leaving a Message on an Answering Machine</u>: Tell who you are and who the message is for. Leave a number where you can be reached and what time the caller can return your call.

"Hi Meghan! I missed you at school today. I hope you're not sick. I have done the homework assignment, in case you want to talk about it. You can call me at 555-1153, before 8:30 tonight. Goodbye!"

5. Your Phone Conversation: Be considerate of other members of your family and the other person's family. Do not call late at night or keep the phone tied up for hours.

> **Kevin:** "Hey Tom, what's up?"
> **Tom:** "Just watching a little TV."
> **Kevin:** "Want to practice ball in a while?"
> **Tom:** "Sure, come over in about 30 minutes!"
> **Kevin:** "Great, see you then. Goodbye!"
> **Tom:** "Goodbye!"

Was there closure in their conversation? Remember to say hello and goodbye!

Attitude = Gratitude!

*Name 10 *people* you are grateful for.

*Name 10 things you are grateful for.

Have you told these people what they mean to you? Let's talk about ways you can show others that you appreciate them!

What Does Attitude Mean?

Attitude has many meanings. How does attitude play an important role in our lives? Why is it important?

   *Attitude is a person's way of looking at life.
   *An attitude can be either positive or negative.
   *Attitude affects a person's posture and the way we carry ourselves.
What messages do you send when your shoulders are slumped? What are you saying about yourself when you stand tall, with a good straight posture? What does a smile say? What does a frown say?

34

Your attitude also affects how well you work, create, or accomplish things. Can you think of ways your attitude can affect what you do or say? How does your attitude affect others? Does your attitude attract friends or drive them away?

Rate your attitude on a scale of 1 to 5, with 1 being poor and 5 being excellent. What can we do to improve our attitudes?

If you need work on your attitude, start with a *"Hello you wonderful you"* in the mirror as you get dressed in the morning. Keep that same positive attitude through the day. Don't let the little things bother you. When you keep positive thoughts in your mind, you will naturally have a wonderful attitude about life! You will be someone your friends will want to be around!

Check Your Attitude

Exercise 1
Jimmy needs to check his attitude.

David: "Hey Jason, have you noticed the way Jimmy is acting lately? He is so strange! He used to be a lot of fun, but now he doesn't want to hang out or have fun with us anymore! His attitude has changed. Something seems weird!"

Jason: "Yeah, I think he might be getting a big head or something. Girls are fun, but what about us guys? We used to hang out and play ball all the time."

David: "Well, let's face it, you're not as pretty as a girl!" (they both laugh) He knows he's good looking and all the girls like to hang around him."

Jason: "I think he needs some friends to help him get back to his old self!"

David: "I think you're right. Let's get him away from all those girls!"

Exercise 2
Jimmy is flirting with a couple of girls between classes when Jason and David walk by.

Jason: "Hey Jimmy, mind if we have a word with you?"

Jimmy is preoccupied with the girls...
Jimmy: Huh?

David: "We have something important to ask you. Will you excuse us, ladies?" The boys go outside together. "Jimmy, what is with you? You act as though you don't even know Jason and me anymore. You walk around, so stuck up, like we're too beneath you to talk to! Remember us? We're your buddies!"

Jimmy is totally surprised!
Jimmy: What do you mean? I didn't know I was acting like that! I guess I've been a little distracted with all the cute girls in school this year. I didn't mean to cut you guys off. *(Jimmy thinks hard about what his friends just said.)* I guess I have been impressed with myself lately. Girls come and go, but not you guys…you are my friends for life!

Thanks to Jason and David, Jimmy received a quick attitude check before his attitude got out of hand.

Punctuality
Is a Habit You Can Master!

Do you have problems being on time? Are you often late for school or an important event? Can others count on you to get things done? Disorganization is a problem that causes us to be late, forgetful, and unreliable. Let's discuss being punctual and any problems you may have with this issue. Perhaps we can look at ways to help you become a more organized, "on-time" person, prepared to assume any task at hand. It all comes down to self-discipline.

Here are some important suggestions to help you become an organized, punctual, and reliable person:

*Tell yourself that you are an "on-time" person. Make this your mindset.
*Plan to arrive 5 or 10 minutes early.
*Set the alarm early for those morning appointments.
*Go to bed earlier if you are having trouble getting started.

*What you are expected to be somewhere, do not think of other things to be done. Fulfill your commitment then move on to other tasks.

It takes time to create a habit and time to break one, but when you decide to be an "on-time" person, you will increase your self-esteem. Others will value your commitment. Once you master the "on-time" habit, your life will be more organized with less stress.

Exercise in Punctuality

The students at Melrose High School are excited about performing "Phantom of the Opera." Rehearsals have already begun this afternoon and Gene O'Connor (lead character) is 30 minutes late.

Mrs. Harris (director): "Where in the world is Gene? We can't do this scene without him. Does someone have his cell phone number?"

Caroline: "Gene just has a problem with time. He's late to every class. I always hear him running down the hall 15 minutes after class has started. He's always in a rush!"

Mrs. Harris: "Something has to be done about this. We can't have the lead in the play show up late for the curtain! If he doesn't come soon, I may have to make some serious decisions about his role."

The other actors agree with Mrs. Harris.

What do you think about this situation? Do you think Gene has a time problem? Does Gene have an important role in the play? Discuss what issues may be making him late. What do you think Mrs. Harris should do? What advise would you offer Gene to help him become an "on-time" person?

Weekly Lesson Review
Joy

Let's review what we have learned! Fill in on the lines below your answers to the following questions for this week's *Fruit of the Spirit* so you can see to use this in your daily activities.

1. What you have learned about this week's Fruit of the Spirit?

2. List the important character values that you have learned from this week's fruit.

    a.

    b

    c.

    d.

    e.

3. Describe five skills that you will use to demonstrate your knowledge of this week's fruit.

    a.

    b.

    c.

    d.

    e.

(Hints: What makes you happy? What does joy mean to you? How can you bring joy to others? How can you be joyful when you are sad?)

God gives us the fruits of the spirit to help us balance out the way we live.

*That includes the way we **think**, the way we **act**, and the way we **treat others** and **ourselves**.*

It also means that when we "chew on the fruits" every day we are living our lives like Jesus!

This week
I want to give my
Joy
by:

Praying to God

Singing Songs of Joyful Praise

Reading the Bible

Memorizing my weekly scripture in my heart

Going to church

Helping Someone

Having a positive attitude

Being joyful when I'm happy

Being joyful when I'm sad

Sharing the Joy of Jesus

Week Three
Fruit of the Spirit:
Peace

Live
in
Peace

Week Three

Begin the Day with Prayer

This Apostle's Pledge:
"I Pledge Allegiance to You, Lord Jesus,
I will walk in Your Grace and Peace.
Create in me Your Temple, Lord, where You
Will want to be.
Make my life Your Vessel
Fill me with Your Living Word
So I can go and share Your Love
With those who haven't heard."

Acts of Grace: Thank You, Please, You're Welcome, Excuse Me

Fruit for the Week: *Peace*

Practicing Peace Exercises

Sing Songs of Praise

Topics:

> **True Obedience**
> **Rude is Crude, Polite is Nice**
> **Tactfulness**
> **Good Sportsmanship**

Fruit for Memory:

> **"Peace I leave you; My Peace, I give you. I do not give you**
> **as the world gives. Do not let your hearts be troubled and do**
> **not be afraid." John 14:27**

True Obedience
Is Worth Mastering

What does true obedience mean? The Bible teaches us that true obedience is *immediate*. How good are you at obeying your parents right away? Let's read Psalm 119:60:

"I will hasten and not delay your commands."

When you give your heart to Jesus, you become a child of God. You are given the gift of salvation. Do you know what salvation means? Let's talk about it. Jesus died for you, so you will want to obey God's commandments. Ask God to help you obey Him, starting today.

Fill in the Blanks:

What was a good example of obedience in the Old Testament? Let's turn to the book of Genesis, Chapter 6.

This is the story of _____ and the specific instructions God gave him.

What did God ask him to build?_____

If Noah had decided to disobey God and build his ark the way he wanted to, what might have been the consequences? It could have meant _____ to Noah, his family, and the animals. The story of Noah teaches us that we cannot obey God *in part*.

Take an honest look at your life. Are you truly obedient to the Lord? Do you practice what you know is right? Are you truly obedient to your parents? Turn to the book of Ephesians, Chapter 5, and see what God has to say about fathers and mothers. What does He say about children?

Parents are not perfect and neither are you. What you learn from your parents in life comes from God. What you learn from their authority will prepare you to respect other authorities in life, such as teachers, police officers, or pastors. If your parents expect you to do a chore, but you would rather do it when you "feel like it", *check your attitude*. Do the task and finish it. You will like yourself for practicing immediate obedience and your parents will respect your behavior. This is called "True Obedience" and it is worth mastering.

True Obedience
Weekly Chart List

Let's create a weekly chart that will test your immediate obedience and your attitude while finishing what you are supposed to do on time! We'll start with Monday and go throughout the week.

- List the chores you are asked to do during the week.

- Fill in the expected ones first and think of more you can do to be helpful.

- At the end of the day, put a check by the ones you completed. (You might want to keep your list on the refrigerator so you can see it.)

- You parents might consider giving you an award for your good attitude and hard work, but if they don't remember that God will reward you in many ways. You will have gained *true obedience*, self-respect, and your parent's respect for you!

Monday:_____

Tuesday:_____

Wednesday:_____

Thursday:_____

Friday:_____

Saturday:_____

Sunday:_____(ask if this can be a day of rest)

Sometimes it's fun to do a chore or do something "special" and not tell a soul you did it. It makes you feel good inside!

Rude is Crude
&
Polite is Nice

This is a really interesting topic and one we need to give some serious attention. Look around at our world at the way people talk and react to each other. What is your opinion of how we treat each other in America? I would like us to take a rude and crude evaluation test of our society, but first, let's examine *rudeness* and *crudeness*, and see what these words means.

Rudeness and crudeness are *negative attitudes* centered around one's own selfishness and one's own agenda. Webster says that these behaviors are unrefined, discourteous, primitive, and void of grace. Being rude or crude is "gross" behavior, whether it is spoken or acted out. Remember students, there is NEVER an appropriate time for rude or crude behavior!

Having a dirty mouth used to be a rare thing. People never "cussed". However, blue language (off color or bad) is used by children, teenagers and adults almost everywhere today.

Here are a few examples of America's behavior in the 21st century. On a scale of 1 to 10, let's score the way people treat each other with an evaluation test. (1 is the lowest; 5 is moderate, and 10 is highest).

- People not smiling at each other

- Helping to carry something for someone

- Going the extra mile

- Making fun (elderly or disabled people)

- Impatience (When you want things done now; traffic jams)

- No love for America

- Lack of respect for Authority

- Selfish Attitudes

- Materialism vs. Sharing and Giving

- Caring for the homeless and sick

- Bad language at the supermarket, department stores

- Bad language at school in the hallways, after school, at football practice, band practice

- Off color conversations on cell phones in public

- Actors and dialogue in movies and television, radio talk shows

- Comments about someone's weight, hair, intelligence, job

Can you think of other examples?

Words can be vicious. From our little mouths can come hurting, stabbing, and *demeaning* ("put downs") language. Turn your Bible to Matthew 24:35. Jesus has something very important to teach us about words. What does Jesus say about judging others in Matthew 7:1?

Apostle Paul tells us in Ephesians 4:29 and 31 important lessons about words. There are several points to these verses. What do they say to you? How vital is it to be aware of the words we speak to others and especially the way we treat them? Paul tells us to be imitators of _____ in Ephesians 5:1-12. Why?

This is a wonderful prayer to begin each day and commit to your heart: *"Let the words of my mouth and the meditation of my heart be acceptable in thy sight, Oh Lord, my strength and my Redeemer."*

Jesus and the Apostle Paul have a lot to teach us on this subject. When God made the world, how did He do it? He did it with the *power* of *His Words*. God spoke and suddenly there was life! Words are the most important tools of expression. They are powerful. We can build or destroy with words.

Jesus wants us to use words of kindness and words that express patience and understanding. To be a *true quality person* walking with Christ, we must be careful of our thoughts and actions. We must use gentle, caring words. Notice how others respond to you in a positive manner! You can influence others to be kind and considerate. Instead of rude and crude, the world will be polite and nice! I am counting on you to do this because you are a *God's Best Is Me* student.

Rude is Crude Exercises

Exercise 1

You and your friends are standing in a very long line to see a great movie. You have been waiting patiently for at least 30 minutes. All of a sudden, a young boy pushes in front of you and shoves you out of place. He does not say "excuse me" or "I'm sorry."

What do you think? How do you and your friends react? He was obviously rude, so what can you suggest for him? Let's give examples of other situations where you have seen people being rude or crude.

Exercise 2

A sister and brother have one computer and right now, Jamie is on line, studying information for her term paper. Her brother, Gary, wants his turn on the computer now!

Gary: "Hey Jamie, get off the computer! It's my turn! You've been on it for hours and I want to 'IM' my friend! You're not gonna get that paper done, anyway!"

Jamie: "Wait just a few more minutes, okay? I just need to study one more topic. By the way, thanks a lot for your kind words and patience, Gary!"

What are your thoughts about this scenario? Should Jamie have gotten off the computer right away? Was she on there too long? Should they have had a time limit set for each of them to use the computer? Was Gary rude or crude? Why? What are some suggestions that will help them respect each other's time and each other as sister and brother?

Words can be sharp are knives; they can also be kind and tender as a dove. Let's watch the way we speak to each other and make a pact:

Speak and Act with kindness and walk in Grace.

Let's build each other up, not tear each other down!

Tactfulness

Tact is the Way to Act

The word *tactful* is a noun. It has many definitions that are important to us, such as accommodating, careful, sensitive, skillful, agreeable, courteous, and fair. In other words, *tactfulness is the ability to say and do the right thing at the right time.*

Can you think of someone who fits these descriptions? Do you? Of course you do! Being tactful is a natural behavior. **Tact is where it's at!** Do you know why? Let's discuss it!

Why do you think we should focus our attention on the subject of being tactful? Have you noticed how many people in the world have lost their tactfulness? Have you noticed how rude people seem to be and not even know they are being so? Let's check our "Tact Skills" and see how well we treat people in all kinds of situations.

Exercise 1

Linda and Susan are working hard behind the scene for the musical, "The King and I". They hear Tiffany (whose brother Tim is starring in the play) boasting about her brother's talent.

Tiffany: "I think Tim has as much talent as Yul Brynner did in the movie!"

Linda: "Well, maybe he does, but why don't you stop bragging about him all the time! You never give anyone else credit for having any talent except your brother and that's not fair! There are lots of talented kids in the show besides Tim. Maybe you should stop and listen to yourself sometime, Tiffany!"

What do you think of this scenario? What do you think of Tiffany? What do you think of Linda's remark? Was she right in what she said or could she have worded it differently? What would be the right thing to say or do in this situation?

Exercise 2

Maggie has always been a thin little girl, but in the last couple of years she has put on quite a bit of weight. While out shopping with her mother, one of her friends from another school bumps into her and says:

Alexis: "Maggie, is that you? You look so different! You've gained so much weight I didn't recognize you!"

Maggie: (embarrassed) "I guess I have. How have you been? Are you still singing and doing commercials?"

Alexis: "I'm great! My mom is buying me some new clothes to wear for another audition. I have to stay skinny so I can make a great impression. I just can't bear the thought of gaining a pound!"

What do you think of Alexis' remarks? Was she just being casual? Was she tactful? How do you think Maggie handled the situation? What would you have said if you were Alexis? What if you were Maggie? How did Alexis' words make Maggie feel? Let's discuss how tactfulness is important.

We now know three slogans:

"Rude is Crude"
"Polite is Nice"
"Tact is Right"

Words are very powerful, so let's remember that what we say to another person can either build them up or hurt them. Let's always remember to be kind!

Good Sportsmanship

Good sports check their character within.

Are you a good sport? Do you know what it means to be a good sport? Let's take a look at playing sports as an example and see how being a good sport is important. Think of some players on your favorite teams. Are they good sports? Being a good sport tells people a lot about your character, how you play the game, and how you treat others.

Good sports "check their character within" by doing the following:

- Follow the rules of the game.

- Avoid arguments with your opponents, your coach, or officials. Anger gets in the way of your concentration and performance. Stay in control and focus on the game. Have fun!

- Be a team player. Remind your teammates to also have a good attitude!

- Be open to allowing all of the team players the opportunity to play in the game. Be unselfish!

- Always play fair. Never play dirty!

- Never take drugs!

- Listen to the coach and follow instructions.

Good sportsmanship means respecting the other team. If the other team wins, congratulate them! Be **big** inside. Show the winning team that you have character and integrity, and they will respect you. You will respect yourself!

Being a good sport is not just playing the game fairly. It is also being kind and considerate in all areas of your life, no matter the circumstance. Being aware of these character values now will help you build a strong foundation of who you will be as an adult. Being a good sport is being a "Quality Person".

Weekly Lesson Review
Peace

Let's review what we have learned! Fill in on the lines below your answers to the following questions for this week's *Fruit of the Spirit* so you can see to use this in your daily activities.

What you have learned about this week's Fruit of the Spirit?

List the important character values that you have learned from this week's fruit.

a.

b

c.

d.

e.

Describe five skills that you will use to demonstrate your knowledge of this week's fruit.

a.

b.

c.

d.

e.

(Hints: Where do Christians find peace? How can you find peace when your life is upside down? How do you find peace when someone hurts you?)

God gives us the fruits of the spirit to help us balance out the way we live.

*That includes the way we **think**, the way we **act**, and the way we **treat others** and **ourselves**.*

It also means that when we "chew on the fruits" every day we are living our lives like Jesus!

This week
I want to live in *Peace*
by:

Praying for God's Peace

Singing Songs of Peace

Reading the Bible

Memorizing my weekly scripture in my heart

Going to church to learn about God's Peace

Having a Peaceful Attitude

Being still and listening to God

Praying for Peace Within

Praying for Peace Around the World

Sharing the Peace of Jesus

Week Four
Fruit of the Spirit:
Patience

Patience

Comes with

Practice!

Week Four

Begin the Day with Prayer

This Apostle's Pledge:
"I Pledge Allegiance to You, Lord Jesus,
I will walk in Your Grace and Peace.
Create in me Your Temple, Lord, where You
Will want to be.
Make my life Your Vessel
Fill me with Your Living Word
So I can go and share Your Love
With those who haven't heard."

Acts of Grace: Thank You, Please, You're Welcome, Excuse Me

Fruit for the Week: *Patience*

Practicing Joy Exercises

Sing Songs of Praise

Topics:
I Want to be a Quality Person
Respect for God and Authority
Dreams Do Come True

Fruit for Memory:
"Be still before the Lord and wait patiently for Him." Psalms 37:7

What is Etiquette?

What does the word **etiquette** mean? It is a French word that means *conventional or socially acceptable, or required in society or in a profession.*

Let's discuss the many different kinds of etiquette. To begin with, all of etiquette means to be considerate and polite. Here are a few examples we will study in our program:

- Table Manners

- Telephone Etiquette

- Punctuality

- Teacher/Student Etiquette

- Conversational Skills

- Introductions

- Proper Attire

- Writing Letters and Thank You Notes

- Punctuality

- Respect for Authority

- Friendship Etiquette

- Good Sportsmanship

- Tactfulness

- Manners Everywhere

- Being a Lady/Being a Gentleman

- Saying "Please", "Thank You", "You're Welcome" and "Excuse Me"

What is Integrity?

What does the word **integrity** mean? It is a noun that means *completeness, wholeness, soundness, sincerity, and honesty.*

Do you think integrity is important? Let's discuss it. Who can you think of that has high integrity? Would you model yourself after this person? How do you feel about your own integrity? Do you try to always do what you say you will do? Be honest! Are you a dependable person? Do you have trouble getting yourself organized or being on time? Are you a true friend? If you can truthfully say, "yes, I am a good friend, I am honest, sincere, and trustworthy", then you can call yourself a person of integrity.

Having integrity is just about the highest quality a person can have! Being a *quality person* is what you should always aim to be. Why? Because in doing so you will have a lot of self-confidence, poise, and self-respect as a result of having integrity. You will love who you are and that is a wonderful feeling to have inside. Remembering to live and to care for others with a sincere heart will help you to live your life with humility and grace.

Who is a Quality Person?

A quality person practices *good etiquette* and has *integrity*. Let's take a look at the character traits of a quality person. How different are they from our list of "rude is crude"? Compare them and see which traits you might need to work on and those you think you already possess.

How do you think we could be a good influence on the people we know who need to change their behaviors? Should we care? Think about this. *Everyone* is important to God. Does it matter to God how each of us think and behave? Does it matter how we treat each other? Some of us may need to be a friend to someone who needs a real quality person to be an example for her or him. In time that person may become a person of integrity just like you!

The Meaning of a Quality Person

Why <u>You</u> Want to be One

We have learned that there are several different kinds of etiquette. We have also learned the definition of integrity. Being a "Quality Person" means that you have a deep respect for yourself and you value others. It means that no matter what situation you are in, you will always use good judgment.

A "Quality Person" has a servant's heart; you willingly make yourself available to help others, putting, their needs before your own. What does Jesus tell us to do? There is no place for arrogance or conceit in a quality person's makeup. A quality person is a person of the highest integrity who follows in the footsteps of Jesus and walks with humility and grace. It is very important to understand the difference between people who have the attributes and values of a quality person and those who do *not*.

The following is a list of Character Traits for NON-Quality People; those who are lacking good character and integrity. Do any of these traits seem to fit you? If so, it's time to make a change! Feel free to discuss these traits privately with your teacher or with the class. Remember that this class is about discovering who we are and what God intends for us to be. We are here to *edify* (build each other up!) one another!

- ❏ Influenced by the world
- ❏ Rebellious
- ❏ Resentful
- ❏ Stressed
- ❏ Unkind
- ❏ Stingy/Selfish
- ❏ Fearful
- ❏ Never on Time
- ❏ Untrustworthy
- ❏ Anxious
- ❏ Worried
- ❏ Self-Centered
- ❏ Negative
- ❏ Inconsistent
- ❏ Without Compassion

Can you think of some other NON-Quality character traits that you have observed about other people? Share them with the class.

Let's look at ourselves. Are we perfect? Absolutely not! We all have faults, but it's so much more fun to live with high standards that help to mold us into quality people!

Becoming a Quality Person

The following is a list of the character traits of a Quality Person. A quality person spends time learning and practicing good etiquette with others. A quality person lives by the Ten Commandments. A quality person is one of true character.

Make a check by those traits you feel you have and a circle around those you may need to work on:

- A person with Good Intentions
- A person with Perseverance
- Trustworthy
- Self-Controlled
- Caring/Loving
- Patient
- On Time
- Polite
- Even Tempered/Pleasant
- Thoughtful
- A person with Commitment
- A person with Integrity
- Faithful
- Compassionate/Giving
- Kind
- Dedicated
- Positive
- Gracious
- Wise
- Generous

This workbook is centered around being a quality person. The Apostle Paul tells us to focus our eyes on Jesus, who gives us our help when things seem to be off track. Jesus is our supreme example of thoughtful etiquette, character, and integrity; He is THE Quality Person! Let's keep looking to His example so that he can smile on our efforts to "do the right thing"!

The Many Different Ways
We Can Be Respectful

- Respect God's Word

- Respect God's House

- Respect for Authority and Rules

- Respect for those in Government

- Respect for our Parents

- Respect for Others

- Respect for those Different than Ourselves

- Respect for those with Disabilities

- Respect for the Elderly

- Respect for Visitors in our Home

- Respect for Others by Showing Manners

- Respect for Myself

Respect Exercises

Here is an exercise for your homework this week. Keep a daily "Respect Journal". Share the ways in which you showed respect this week with the class.

1. Show your parents 10 ways that you respect them. (hints: answer yes/no mam or sir each time you are asked to do a chore, finish your chore, be obedient, make them a surprise, pick a rose for your mom, pop some popcorn for dad!)

2. Do something special around the house to show you care. (hints: take out the garbage, help bring in the groceries, help your little brother or sister with homework, share your computer time)

3. Answer respectfully to all adults. (hints: yes/no mam or sir to teachers, pastors, aunts, uncles, friends of parents, police officers)

4. Help an elderly person. (hints: roll a wheel chair, help carry in groceries, answer the phone, help with gardening)

5. Be quiet and attentive in church. (hints: listen to the sermon, take notes on the lesson, walk quietly in the halls, greet everyone with a smile, tell your Sunday school teacher or pastor how much you enjoyed and learned from their lesson)

God's Dreams for You

Did you know that long, long ago *you* were a dream? Yes! You were a dream in God's heart. One day He sat down very quietly and began dreaming of you from head to toe…your eyes, your ears, your smile, and every little detail about you. He dreamed of the world where you would live, your parents, brothers and sisters, your friends, and your experiences in life. He put his creative spirit inside your heart so that you could enjoy expressing the special gifts He planned for you to develop to your highest potentials.

God is a creative God. Look all around you. He created the moon, the starts, the world, and everything in it! He gave you your very own unique gifts to share with everyone and to glorify Him. You are God's very special dream come true. You are a miracle! Isn't that wonderful?

These quotes inspire us to believe in the beauty of our dreams:

"If you can dream it, you can do it."
Walt Disney

"You can often measure the size of a person by the size of their dreams."
Robert Schueller

"I think we dream so we don't have to be apart so long.
If we're in each other's dreams, we can be together all the time."
Calvin & Hobbs

"Go confidently in the direction of your dreams. Live the life you have imagined."
Henry David Thoreau

"All of our dreams can come true if we have the courage to pursue them."
Walt Disney

"The only thing that will stop you from fulfilling your dreams is you."
Tom Bradley

"Have a dreamer's heart. It will keep you young forever."

Jeanne Sheffield

Dreams Do Come True

God gives us dreams and imaginations so we can look forward to a bright and shining future. God made us in His image to be just like Him. He wants us to come and ask Him what he thinks. He wants us to dream, because many dreams He put into our hearts before we are born. He wants us to know which ones are important so that we can hold on to them as we are growing up.

God asks us to talk to Him all the time because He knows us better than anyone. That is why we turn to Him for wisdom and guidance. When we do, we will be amazed at His surprises! God will take us through the steps we need to take to make our dreams come true when we are obedient to Him.

<u>Answer these questions about your dreams:</u>

What do I dream about?

What am I interested in?

What do I like?

What do I dream about doing this year?

What do I want to do when I grow up?

Where do I want to live when I grow up?

Where do I want to travel?

Do I want to go to college? Where do I want to go to college?

Do I dream that I may have a family one day?

What values have I learned that I may teach my own children?

Do I ask God to make my dreams come true?

Do I ask God to give me things I should have and not just the things I think I want to have?

Do I dream that I can change the world?

How could I change the world to make it better?

Do I ask God for too much or do I ask Him for too little?

Do I believe that dreams do come true?

On a separate sheet of paper, draw a picture of "My Dream House". Write about your dream house.

<u>Special Project:</u>

Let's make a "Dream Poster" and put your dreams into action!

Weekly Lesson Review
Patience

Let's review what we have learned! Fill in on the lines below your answers to the following questions for this week's *Fruit of the Spirit* so you can see to use this in your daily activities.

1. What you have learned about this week's Fruit of the Spirit?

2. List the important character values that you have learned from this week's fruit.

a.

b

c.

d.

e.

3. Describe five skills that you will use to demonstrate your knowledge of this week's fruit.

a.

b.

c.

d.

e.

___

(Hints: What does patience mean? How can we be patient when we are really excited about something? How do we show our patience with our younger friends, brothers, and sisters?)

God gives us the fruits of the spirit to help us balance out the way we live.

*That includes the way we **think**, the way we **act**, and the way we **treat others** and **ourselves**.*

It also means that when we "chew on the fruits" every day we are living our lives like Jesus!

This week
I want to Show My
Patience
by:

Praying to God

Singing Songs of Patience

Reading the Bible

Memorizing my weekly scripture in my heart

Going to church to learn about God's Patience

Having a Patient Attitude

Being more Patient with Others

Being more Patient with Myself

Being Forgiving

Sharing the Patience of Jesus

Week Five
Fruit of the Spirit: Kindness

Love

to be

Kind

Week Five

Begin the Day with Prayer

This Apostle's Pledge:
"I Pledge Allegiance to You, Lord Jesus,
I will walk in Your Grace and Peace.
Create in me Your Temple, Lord, where You
Will want to be.
Make my life Your Vessel
Fill me with Your Living Word
So I can go and share Your Love
With those who haven't heard."

Acts of Grace: Thank You, Please, You're Welcome, Excuse Me

Fruit for the Week: *Kindness*

Practicing Joy Exercises

Sing Songs of Praise

Topics:

> *Being a Lady*
> *Being a Gentleman*
> *Writing Notes*
> *Jealousy Can Eat You Up*

Fruit for Memory:

> *"Pleasant words are a honeycomb sweet to the soul and*
> *healing to the bones." Proverbs 16:14*

Being a Lady

Who would you say is a perfect lady? What qualities does she have? Do you want to grow up to be like her? Being a lady starts from within. The secret of happiness is liking who you are and valuing who you are. Did you know that a beautiful spirit shows on the outside even more than a pretty smile? It means much more to be someone who loves herself, not in a conceited way, but in a thankful way. You will begin to watch how people are drawn to you and how wonderful you will feel inside.

Here are some guidelines to follow and maybe we will think of other ideas to add to your development as we go along:

- Have a Cheerful Spirit...........Smile!

- Choose Positive Friends who Share your Values

- Listen to what Others have to say

- Be a Thoughtful Friend

- Be Obedient to God and your Parents

- Be Honest with Yourself

- Have a Caring Heart

- Dress Modestly and look like a Lady

- Stand with Good Posture

- Be Gracious to everyone, especially in your home

- Expect a Gentleman to open doors for you

- Eat Nutritious Food and Drink lots of Water

- Exercise at least 3 times per week

- Use a good Skin and Hair Care program

- Stay out of the sun; use self-tanning lotion to tan fair skin

- Keep your Nails Manicured

- Don't listen to off color jokes

- Don't watch violent television show/movies or those containing sexually explicit material

- Talk pleasantly on the phone and take messages carefully

- Never call boys, no matter what your friends may say or do

- Remember to write thank you, sympathy, & congratulation notes

- Remember your table manners, how to set a table, and what each utensil is used for

These are only a few important tips for being a lady. There are plenty more topics to add for you to be a lady of poise and grace. Can you think of more things you have observed about a lady you admire?

Girls, things have changed a lot since Amy Vanderbilt wrote her famous book on etiquette, but some thinks remain solidly constant. One of these things is how girls often make the mistake of "pursuing boys". Wait for that cute boy to call you. In the mean time, keep yourself busy. This is the wisdom of your grandmothers. Follow their advice and see what happens!

Being a Gentleman

Who is the best example of a true gentleman in your life? Is it your father or your grandfather? Is it a teacher or a friend? What is it about that person that makes you admire them? Being a gentleman requires a lot of responsibility and here are some ways that will help you become a true gentleman.

- Have a Cheerful Spirit…Smile!

- Stand Tall with good Posture

- Be a True Friend

- Obey God and Your Parents

- Wear the Right Look for the Right Occasion

- Ladies are always First

- Open Doors for Ladies

- Offer your Seat to Ladies

- Stand when a Lady enters the room or joins you at the table

- Be Courteous to Elderly People

- Be a Good Sport when someone else wins

- Have a Good Attitude

- Be a Good Team Player

- Offer a Handshake when being Introduced

- Learn to set a table

- Learn the use of each utensil

- Learn how to tip and when to tip

- Eat nutritious foods instead of junk food

- Drink lots of water

- Use a good skin and hair care program

- Use good manners when talking on the phone and taking messages

- Show Consideration

Learning how to be a gentleman is important and putting your manners into motion is fun!

Writing Notes

Tips and Ideas!

Have you ever written a thank you note or a birthday card? If you haven't, you need to know that writing personal notes is a lot of fun and can be very expressive!

Before we begin creating ideas together, let's talk about writing a thank you note. Why should you write someone who did something nice or special for you? Is it enough just to *say* "thank you" when someone gives you a gift? Should you just *email* a quick thanks? Should you just buy a pre-written card and just scribble your name?

No! All the above is terribly impersonal and basically rude. What you need to realize is that if someone has taken the time to think about you, shop for you, and spend money on you, YOU must *acknowledge* their thoughtfulness! If someone were to send you something breakable in the mail, would you call upon receiving the gift? Friends want to know if their gifts arrived safely. Show them you are appreciative and do it as soon as possible after the gift arrives.

There are beautiful, funny, and clever thank you notes in stores. Start collecting your very own and have them ready for use when you feel the need to write someone.

Examples of Thank You Notes

Today we are going to create our own thank you notes and notes for special occasions. Here are a few examples that will give you some ideas about how to write them:

<u>Girls</u>

Dear Aunt Carol,

    Thank you so much for my beautiful new cross necklace. I did not have one until now. I have gotten several compliments, so I'll probably wear it every day. Thank you, Aunt Carol, for being so sweet!

Love,

Leah

<u>Boys</u>

Dear Grandpa,

Thank you for my new fishing rod. It is awesome! It's just want I wanted. I can't wait to go fishing with you next summer. I bet we'll catch a lot of bass! Thanks again!

Love,

Jerry

Notice that Leah and Jerry thanked their gift-givers twice. It is very nice to tell the giver thank you at the start of your letter and at the end. Why? Because it lets them know that you are sincerely grateful.

Suggestions for Writing Notes

Here are some tips to help you write good notes:

- *Find a good writing pen and notepaper that is appropriate for the occasion. Write your note at a clean, level table or desk.*

- *Never write when you are tired or in a hurry. When you have the person in your thoughts, sit down and write what you want to say to that person. You may consider using a scratch pad first so you won't make a mistake when writing the actual letter.*

- *Write a note to the person that says you are really thinking about her or him. For example, instead of just signing your name on a birthday card, you might write a special "Happy Birthday, Enjoy Your Day" message that let's them know you really are thinking of them on that special day!*

- *Write the card ahead of time so that it will arrive on the person's special day. Keep a calendar handy and write in all the special dates of your family and friends.*

- *Be real and natural in your message so that your note sounds sincere.*

- *Write a note within a week to 10 days to acknowledge your given. Do not wait too long. You do not want the gift-giver to think you never received the gift or don't care for the gift. Remember the Golden Rule, "Treat others the way you want to be treated."*

- *Be sure to send a note to grandparents and other relatives for special gifts and treats.*

There are all kinds of occasions when we want to write a note to someone. What are some special occasions to remember? What are some other reasons to send special notes? Share this information with your friends and let them know that writing notes makes you feel good about who you are!

- *Let's create a Get Well card. What are some thoughts you could say to someone who is sick or going into the hospital?*

- *Let's write a Congratulations card. What kinds of graduations are there? What are some other reasons why people receive congratulations?*

- *Mother's Day and Father's Day cards. What can you write to your parents to say how much they mean to you?*

Jealousy Can Eat You Up

What exactly is jealousy? Jealousy is ill-feelings toward someone who receives, does, or possesses something we wish for ourselves. This kind of feeling is common to people of all ages, races, and religions. The good news is that jealousy is easy to overcome!

What happens with the first bite of jealousy? We may begin to have negative or unconscious thoughts about someone. Those thoughts then play over and over in our conscious minds, like an old tape! The person may not have any idea that you feel this way about her or him. How do you feel inside? It is *not* a pleasant feeling, is it? Jealousy is not fun. It is uncomfortable and unnatural. Jealousy is not intended to be part of our lives.

Jealousy is also a sign of *immaturity*. When we are small children, jealousy enters our lives. We feel jealous if a sister or brother gets more attention than we do from our parents. We become jealous if a teacher pays more attention to another student in class. We get jealous if we don't win first place. We are jealous if our best friend was chosen cheerleader and we weren't. The list of jealousies goes on!

God did not give us a sense of jealousy. He gave us the choice to find our identity in Him. When we become secure in all the gifts God intends for us in this life, we will be happy and want for others to be happy in whatever achievements they may attain!

Ways to End Jealousy

1. *Stop comparing yourself with others!* You are God's own special creation. You have your own special gifts to offer this world. There is plenty of space in this world for you to make your own mark in your own time!

2. *Have patience and wait for the Lord!* There is a reason for everything and now is the time to grow and learn. You must absorb all that is around you so that you will be ready when your time comes! God knows your needs better than you. Ask Him to remove any spirit of jealousy in your heart. Pray for Him to give you a fresh, new spirit to accept others for their journeys in life as well as your own.

3. *Want for all people to fulfill their destinies and be successful.* Turn to Jeremiah 29:11 in your Bible and see the plans God has for you. It is exciting to know that we can totally depend on Him to guide us to reach our goals.

What has been your own experience with jealousy? Were you the person who was jealous? Have you been hurt by a friend's jealousy of you? Let's share these experiences and how we felt. If you could go back to that moment in time, do you think you might have a different attitude? Let's talk about how we can change that experience now that you understand what jealousy is.

As we leave this topic, I want you all to remember that when we have a sense of who we are and the realization of our own "unique purpose" to fulfill, we do not have to compare ourselves with others. Our purpose in life is to follow God's commands, not covet others. God wants us to enjoy the journey of discovering life every day!

Exercises in Jealousy

Exercise 1.

Why Jealousy Can Eat You Up: Paul and Linda have beautiful voices. Today is an exciting day because they are entering the finals at the Youth Talent Fair Competitions. They are singing a duet from "Phantom of the Opera". Michael and Carla, another duo, are competing with a beautiful country medley. Let's see what goes on behind the scenes between Carla and Michael while Paul and Linda are performing.

Carla: "Wow, she really has a high voice! I think she sings off key, don't you? And look at that dress! It's way too old for her with all those sequins. Wait until they hear us! We're going to knock the crowd off their feet! They don't stand a chance next to us!"

Michael: "Yeah, we've got it made! Who wants to hear that old opera stuff, anyway!"

What does this dialogue say about Carla and Michael? Are they jealous? What could we suggest to them to have a better attitude about competition? How would Paul and Linda feel if they heard their comments?

Wishing Others the Best: Allison is traveling to Europe and will visit friends in England for the summer. This is a new opportunity for her. Allison's best friend, Carrie, has no brothers or sisters and it will be hard to part with Allison for 2 months. How do you think Carrie will handle saying goodbye?

Allison answers the door bell. Carrie is there holding a gift: "Hi Carrie! A present for me?!"

Carrie: "I was thinking about your trip and since you're going to be away for the summer, I thought you might like a journal. You can write about all the neat stuff that happens...what you see, who you meet, where you go! Then you can read it to me when you get back!"

Allison: "Carrie, you are the best friend in the world! This is great! Sure, of course, I'll share everything with you...you're my best friend. I would never have thought of taking a journal. I can't wait to see what these pages will say!"

Carrie: "And don't forget to take a lot of pictures, too! I want to pretend I was there with you!"

Do you sense any jealousy in this scene? Could Carrie be jealous of Allison's trip to Europe? Would you call this a caring friendship? What makes this farewell better than one filled with jealousy?

When we are secure about who we are inside there is no need or "room" for jealousy. We have already discussed that jealousy is a sign of _immaturity._ Being secure with who we are means that we have a big heart to wish the very best for everyone, especially our best friends. What a wonder feeling to have inside!

Weekly Lesson Review

Kindness

Let's review what we have learned! Fill in on the lines below your answers to the following questions for this week's *Fruit of the Spirit* so you can see to use this in your daily activities.

1. What you have learned about this week's Fruit of the Spirit?

2. List the important character values that you have learned from this week's fruit.

   a.

   b

   c.

   d.

   e.

3. Describe five skills that you will use to demonstrate your knowledge of this week's fruit.

   a.

   b.

   c.

   d.

   e.

(Hints: How can I show kindness to my family, friends, and neighbors? What does Jesus say about kindness? How do I show my kindness to someone who is not kind to me?)

God gives us the fruits of the spirit to help us balance out the way we live.

*That includes the way we **think**, the way we **act**, and the way we **treat others** and **ourselves**.*

It also means that when we "chew on the fruits" every day we are living our lives like Jesus!

This week
I want to be
Kind
by:

Praying for God's Kindness

Singing Songs of Kindness

Reading the Bible

Memorizing my weekly scripture in my heart

Going to church to learn about God's Kindness

Having a Kind Attitude

Finding Ways to be Kind to Others

Thinking about God's Kindness to All of Us

Going out of my way to be Kind

Surprising someone with a Kind Gesture

Sharing the Kindness of Jesus

Week Six
Fruit of the Spirit:
Goodness

Be a

Package

Of

Goodness

Week Six

Begin the Day with Prayer

This Apostle's Pledge:
"I Pledge Allegiance to You, Lord Jesus,
I will walk in Your Grace and Peace.
Create in me Your Temple, Lord, where You
Will want to be.
Make my life Your Vessel
Fill me with Your Living Word
So I can go and share Your Love
With those who haven't heard."

Acts of Grace: Thank You, Please, You're Welcome, Excuse Me

Fruit for the Week: *Goodness*

Practicing Joy Exercises

Sing Songs of Praise

Topics:

Table Manners
Manners Everywhere
Temptation is an Opportunity
The Helmet of Salvation
What Have We Learned Together?

Fruit for Memory:

"A merry heart doeth good like medicine."
Proverbs 17:22

Table Manners

Why are table manners important? Who do you know that has good table manners? Do you? Having good table manners says a lot about the way we are raised. People notice if you sit at a table and show good manners. One day, you might be invited to have dinner with the President of the United States and you will want to be prepared and confident!

Here are some basic rules to help you get started:

- Do not start eating before everyone is seated.
- At a formal dinner, wait to see if the hostess has a special seat for you. You may look for a place card at the table with your name.
- Do not start eating until the hostess has started. Then begin eating with the same utensils.
- Chew with your mouth closed. Chew slowly.
- Never talk with food in your mouth!
- Sit up straight. Do not lean over your plate.
- Do not put your elbows on the table.
- Keep your napkin in your lap!
- Never scrape the plate with your fork. Never lick a bowl or plate!
- Do not use your fingers to put food on your fork.
- Please do not lick the knife! This is rude and dangerous!
- If thirsty, you may ask for a refill, but do not gulp your drink.
- Do not slurp your soup or your drink.
- Ask quietly to be excused from the table if you need to go to the bathroom. Do not blow your nose at the table.
- When everyone has finished eating, place your napkin to the left of your plate. Put your silverware at a diagonal across your plate.
- Pass the salt and pepper together when asked.
- Boys do not wear hats at the table except for religious reasons.
- Girls may wear hats for Ladies Luncheons or Teas.
- Boys always help ladies into their chairs and when they get up from the table.

I Am a Quality Person with Good Manners

In Public and On Trips

Here are some important courtesies you as a "Quality Person" should extend to everyone, regardless of whether you know them or not:

Be humble. Put others first, yourself last. The Bible teaches "the first shall be last and the last shall be first."

Be courteous. Remember the Golden Rule: "Do unto others the way you would have them do unto you."

Behave yourself. Do not be loud, rude, or cause a commotion in public. Do not run in the hallways at school, church, or other public places. Save your energy for the outdoors! Walk and talk gracefully in public and show your respect as a guest in someone's home.

Be friendly. Introduce yourself if you have not been introduced. Be sociable and neighborly. The Bible teaches us in the second commandment to "_____ *thy neighbor as* _____."

Be modest. Practice modesty in all situations. Never take your life and its value for granted. Be grateful for any compliment you receive. Do not act as if you are better than anyone else is; *God made us equal.*

On trips: Pack your clothes ahead of time. Choose clothes that match, that are interchangeable and suitable for the occasion. Do not over pack; less is best. Remember all your toiletries and books. Go to the bathroom before leaving.

Be respectful to the driver. Do not be disruptive with other passengers in the back seat. The driver has your life as well as others in his or her hands. Driving a car is a very serious matter, especially when others are on board.

Practice the fundamentals you have learned, even if you are in a foreign country. You will want everyone who meets you to think that Americans are kind, friendly, and considerate people. Show everyone that you are a true **"Quality Person"**.

Temptation is an Opportunity

"Happy is the man who doesn't give in and do wrong when he is tempted, for afterwards he will get as his reward the crown of life that God has promised those who love him."
James 1:12

Of all the topics we have studied in your *God's Best Is Me* manual, I believe temptation is the most important topic for you to study. Young people are growing up in a self-serving world. You need a mentor like Apostle Paul to guide you, direct you, and correct you. As we read Paul's writings, he makes it clear how we should handle temptation even in the 21st century.

Do you know that every temptation is an opportunity to do good? Do you know that it can be as easy to do the right thing as the wrong thing? Temptation is there to provide you a *choice*. Satan wants to tear you down, but God wants to develop you. When you choose to do His will instead of Satan's, you are growing in the *character of Christ*.

You may be asking, "how do I stay away from temptation?" Doing it on your own is not easy. We first need to look at the qualities of Christ's character. There are nine of them. Can you name them? They are called the *fruits of the spirit* and each of them describes Jesus: **Love, Joy, Peace, Patience, Kindness, Goodness, Faithfulness, Gentleness, and Self-Control!**

The fruits of the spirit are an expansion of the Ten Commandments! They portray a beautiful picture of Jesus as the perfect example for each fruit. God helps you to develop these fruits in your life so that you will have the strength to fight temptation. As you grow in character, you will be tempted, but when you call upon the Holy Spirit, He will help you to make the right choice. Read God's Word every day and put on the "Helmet of Salvation", which is the full armor of God. Think of yourself as a knight covered in armor, ready for battle! It's fun learn and express the Helmet of Salvation together. Let's do it!

The Helmet of Salvation

"I stand firm with the belt of truth buckled around my waist,
with the breastplate of righteousness in place,
and with my shoes fitted with the gospel of peace.
I now take up the shield of faith
to extinguish all the flaming arrows of the evil one.
I put on the helmet of salvation and sword of the spirit,
Which is the Word of God."

Ephesians 6:13-17

This is what each position means:

- The Belt of Truth helps me to see through God's eyes and not to be deceived by Satan's lies.

- The Breastplate of Righteousness helps me to see that I am as righteous to God as Jesus Himself is.

- The Shoes of the Gospel help me realize that I have made total peace with God and I can bring peace to others.

- The Shield of Faith means that God's protection surrounds us even under Satan's vicious attacks.

- The Sword of the Spirit means that God's Word defeats every lie Satan will ever try to tell us.

Jesus was totally dependent on God, in His life and His death. We can ask God to help us to be dependent on Him. We can thank Him that we are on the "winning" side!

Temptation Exercises

We have studied integrity and its meaning. When dealing with temptation, integrity is built by refusing the temptation to be dishonest. Look at this scene and see what happens:

Kelly finds a twenty-dollar bill on the floor of the girls' restroom at school. She stops, looks at it, and thinks:

Kelly: *"Wow! I wonder who lost this. I wish I hadn't found it!"*

What is Kelly concerned about? What do you think she should do? If no one sees her, who would know if she took it? Kelly has a history of shoplifting and has been in Juvenile Detention twice. However, over the past year, she has been studying God's Word and she is determined to do the right thing. Kelly turns to God in prayer and says:

Kelly: *"Lord, I know you see this and I know you want me to do the right thing. Since you came into my life, I feel so much stronger. I know I could keep it, Lord, but I won't. I know you have so much more for me, especially since I want to do what's right."*

Kelly takes the money to her teacher, Mrs. Reid.

Mrs. Reid.*: "Oh Kelly, I am so glad you found it! It must have fallen out of my purse. I have to go to the grocery store today, thank you for being honest. I am so proud of you!"*

What would you do? What does it take to do the right thing? We can do what is right when we have integrity, a conscience, and an awareness that God is always with us. In what ways have you been tempted? Did you give in or turn away? How did you feel when you resisted or when you gave in to temptation? Remember it is always *our choice.*

What does God say to us about keeping our bodies holy? How does He feel about what we put into our bodies? What does He think about cigarettes or alcohol? What does God say about sexual sin? Is God aware of what we do in private? He tells us He knows every hair on our heads. He is extremely aware of us and He *cares about us!*

Apostle Paul gives important instruction to us in 1 Corinthians 6:16. He gives us firm instructions about sexual behavior outside of marriage. What does Apostle Paul mean when he says we were bought with a price? When we give our lives to Jesus, to whom do we belong? Do we continue to think and behave like the rest of the world or are we as Christians separate and set apart?

<u>These are the Steps in Temptation's Schemes:</u>

- <u>Desire</u>: Satan's tricks are the same. He may give you the desire for revenge, to bully someone, or to try drugs, alcohol, and cigarettes. Satan tempts us with words like, "Come on, you deserve it! Do it! It's exciting! It's fun! It's now or never!" The book of James tells us there is "a whole army of evil desires within you."

- <u>Doubt</u>: Satan tries to tell you to doubt what God has taught you about sin. The Bible warns us, "Watch out! Don't let evil thoughts or doubts make any of you turn from the living God."

- <u>Deception</u>: Satan is known as the father of deception. Satan tells young people today, "Go ahead, everyone is doing it. You'll be cool and that's what matters. It's only a little sin. Who cares? You're not hurting anyone. God won't even notice!" However, a little sin is like being a little bit pregnant. It will eventually show.

- <u>Disobedience</u>: Let's look at the Ten Commandments in Deuteronomy 5:6-21. What temptations do you see? Do you think God was just making a few suggestions? God's commandments are His laws and He means business. He also tells us that when we obey Him, He will be pleased with us and we will feel good about ourselves. Apostle Paul tells us about temptation and how God helps us in 1 Corinthians 10: 12-13.

If you listen to Satan's lies continually, you will fall into his trap. James 1:13-16 gives us a warning: "We are trapped when we are drawn away and trapped by our own evil desires. Then our evil desires conceive and give birth to sin; and sin, when it is full-grown, gives birth to death. Do not be deceived, my dear friends."

<u>Ways that Temptation can be Defeated:</u>

Turn your Bible to 1 Timothy 2:22, then to 1 Corinthians 10:13. With God there is always a way out. Sometimes you may feel that you cannot resist being tempted, but that is Satan's lie trying to bind you. Remember to turn to God. He is always faithful and will help you resist the enemy.

- <u>Refocus your attention</u>: Find another idea. Read God's Word. Nothing can help you more. Once your mind is on something else, temptation loses its power.

- <u>Tell a friend about your struggle</u>: We all need a friend to turn to who will care about our fears or struggles. Pray to the Lord. He already knows, but He wants you to confide and trust in Him.

- <u>Resist the Devil</u>: Turn to James 4:7. What will the devil do when we resist him? If you believe in Jesus, Satan cannot *make* you do anything. He can only suggest. Be wise and discerning about situations and people you meet. The devil comes in many disguises and you must be sharp enough to catch him. Never argue with the devil. He has had too much practice. Instead, use the Word of God against him. Memorize scripture so that you will have plenty of bullet power to nail him to the ground!

- <u>Memorize one verse of scripture each week for the rest of your life</u>: Use a chalkboard with chalk or an erasable board with erasable markers and write a verse on it each week. It works! You will have scriptures carved in your heart, ready to speak when someone needs them. You will be amazed at your own strength of character as you put on your shield of protection with the "Helmet of Salvation". You will have the power of God to resist Satan in all his devious (underhanded) topics. May God's Force be with you!

Weekly Lesson Review

Goodness

Let's review what we have learned! Fill in on the lines below your answers to the following questions for this week's *Fruit of the Spirit* so you can see to use this in your daily activities.

1. What you have learned about this week's Fruit of the Spirit?

2. List the important character values that you have learned from this week's fruit.

   a.

   b

   c.

   d.

   e.

3. Describe five skills that you will use to demonstrate your knowledge of this week's fruit.

   a.

   b.

   c.

   d.

   e.

(Hints: How can I show my goodness to others? How do I choose between what is good and what is bad?)

God gives us the fruits of the spirit to help us balance out the way we live.

*That includes the way we **think**, the way we **act**, and the way we **treat others** and **ourselves**.*

It also means that when we "chew on the fruits" every day we are living our lives like Jesus!

This week
I want to be
Good
by

Praying for God's Goodness

Singing Songs of Goodness

Reading the Bible

Memorizing my weekly scripture in my heart

Going to church to learn about God's Goodness

Having a Good Attitude

Desiring God's Goodness in Me

Looking for the Goodness in Others

Thinking God is Good All the Time

Being a Package of Goodness to Everyone

Sharing the Goodness of Jesus

❧ ✦✦✦✦ ❧

Elective Topics

❧ ✦✦✦✦ ❧

The following three topics are optional, dependent upon your time factor and interest:

1. Staying Pure Before God

2. Making Good Choices With Cell Phones

3. Different Cultures & Different Etiquette (Examples: Japan & Kenya)

1. Staying Pure Before God

Starting from early childhood your heavenly Father wants you to understand what *"staying pure before Him"* means. Staying pure means to promise God and yourself to stay innocent, celibate *(kept to ones self)* and clean from sexual sin before marriage.

Living a life of purity is more than just abstaining from sex. It includes what you think about and how you spend your time. Christian purity is a matter of totally committing your life to Christ. It is a commitment of godliness in every area of your life. You are to honor God with your whole being, because His Word says that He gave you your life before He even created the foundations of the world. Yet life is not as innocent as it once was in decades past. Unfortunately for you as children and teenagers, every where you turn you are exposed to sexual images and offensive language. So how can you overcome the world and live a life of purity?

The first way is to be *obedient* to what God tells you in His Word and to realize that obedience is for your benefit. It is *not* meant to restrain you or to hold you back from enjoying life. Obedience to God's commands shows God respect and obedience gives you respect for yourself. Staying sexually pure is for your safety and protection, especially in this world where there are so many sexually transmitted diseases that could cause great harm to your health and destroy your future.

Here are Several Key Steps to Help You Live A Life of Purity:

Pay Attention To How You Dress-

We have already addressed this importance of dressing modestly in our topic called "Modesty Is In." How does dressing modestly help us to live a "Pure life?" How does the way we dress affect the opposite sex when we dress modestly or promiscuously? Are we trying to tempt the opposite sex or are we trying to help their thoughts stay pure? Young males are very visual, so dressing modestly helps them to enjoy who you are as a person and not focus on your physical body. Dressing modestly, yet in style is the best way to dress.

Be Careful of What You Watch And What You Listen To-

Not allowing your eyes and ears to see and hear things that are inappropriate takes careful discipline. It is very hard, especially when you are visually bombarded with sexually explicit television shows and movies. The radio plays off color lyrics to songs and the CD'S and iPods you buy and listen to often use vulgar language. This is why you must be very selective with what you decide is right for your senses to take in.

Listen to wholesome, Godly music. Fill your heart with praise music and sing along with wonderful songs that honor God. Watch for PG movie and television ratings which offer clean language and normal, healthy behaviors on the screen.

Keep Your Standards High-

Never let the world's standards persuade you to do what you know is wrong. Always put God's principles before you. Being a Christian makes you a child of God. This is why He always expects you to be on your very best behavior. Your standards can affect many young people by the words you say and your attitude. When you see a class mate, a friend or boy friend who tries to entice you do something wrong, stand your ground and share with them a scripture that will convict them and help them to turn away from committing that sin. Tell them about your standards and beliefs and how they work for you and how they can help them. Share a scripture that will make them think about their behavior. You may have the blessing of bringing someone to Christ.

Start A Bible Study With Your Girl Friend, Boy Friend or Friends-

Pray together and for each other to stay pure before the Lord. Read the Bible together taking turns reading a chapter aloud to each other. Have a discussion about what you both learned. Let's read what the Bible says about who will inherit the kingdom of God in 1 Corinthians 6:13. By concentrating on the Word of God every day you will discover how much it will help to be strong in your faith and convictions.

Read What God Says About Being Pure-

One of the most beautiful passages in the Bible was written by Apostle Paul to remind us in Philippians 4:8 which says,

"Finally brethren, whatsoever things are true,

whatsoever things are honest,

whatsoever things are just,

whatsoever things are pure,

whatsoever things are lovely,

whatsoever things are of good report;

if there be any virtue, and

if there be any praise,

think on these things."

2 Timothy 2:22 relates a wise passage which says,

"Flee youthful lusts: but follow righteousness, faith, charity, peace,

with them that call on the Lord with a pure heart."

1 Thessalonians 4: 3-4 says,

"God's will is for you to be holy, so stay away from all sexual sin. Then each of you will control his own body and live in holiness and honor."

Galatians 5:16 also says,

"So I say, let the Holy Spirit guide your lives. Then you won't be doing what is sinful nature craves."

Open your Bibles and let's turn to 1 Corinthians 7, 8 & 9. What does God say the body is meant for in these massages? What do you think sexual immorality does to a society? What has it done to America, South America, Europe, Asia, Africa and around the world? Does it destroy personal relationships? Families? Are many children born to young teenagers? Do teenagers lose their own child hoods because of it? Does having children out of wed lock affect your education? Why? Does it break down respect for the opposite sex? Are you taking a big chance on contracting a sexual disease? Could you possibly die because of it? Does it hurt a person's self-worth? Does it cause guilt and shame?

Is it worth it then to have sex out of marriage? Isn't it worth waiting on the Lord to bring you the perfect mate to share your life within marriage? Isn't it worth it to keep your body pure before the Lord? He knows who will be the most compatible person who will share your faith and principles and He will send that person to you at the proper time. When you honor God, He will honor you and shine His light on you and make your paths straight, because of your obedience. Don't live a disobedient life and make the mistakes so many young people have made. Instead, reap the many rewards of living an obedient life. Stay close to your Father who knows you better than any one and He will give you His divine wisdom to know what to do in all situations.

Pray and ask God to help you live a life of purity before Him.

2. Making Good Choices With Cell Phones

You are fortunate to be a part of such exciting times living in the beginning of the 21st century. You are also a part of a highly advanced technological age where communication is advancing literally every moment. What was new a few months ago is out dated today. One of the greatest inventions in communication is the cell phone. This tiny little apparatus has given people ways to communicate that were previously never heard of, let alone dreamed of in decades passed before us.

Since our cell phones play such an integral part of our daily lives, let's take a good look at *how, when, why and where* we should use them. Then we can we have a class discussion.

Let's Start With Several Cell Phone Rules To Follow:

- Always your appropriate language on the cell phone.

- Lower your voice when talking

- Don't speak about personal topics in public.

- Avoid taking calls when in a conversation with someone.

- Do not text when someone is talking to you face-to-face.

- Put your phone's ringer on silent mode in theatres, places of worship, the class room and restaurants.

- Don't light up your phone screen in a dark theatre.

- Do not talk on your cell phone in an elevator.

- Do not talk on your cell phone while driving.

- Don't blame the other person for a dropped call.

- Avoid looking up numbers or look at the internet during a conversation.

- Choose your ring tone wisely. (no annoying, irritating tone)

- Use your text mode to say "Thank You".

- Use your cell phone to call for an emergency or to help someone stranded.

- Always watch your text language. Your message could end up on a Face Book page for the world. You do not want to be embarrassed.

- Find an "on time' and "off time" discipline when using your cell phone.

- Don't let talking or texting on your cell phone become an obsession.

- Find other things to do.

- Maintain at a 10 foot zone from any one while talking on your cell phone.

- Do not answer unknown calls. Let them leave a message.

- Do not answer unknown texts. It could be a spam message.

- Learn how to block others from calling or texting your phone.

- Be careful of what pictures or videos you put on the internet.

- Be aware of your environment and remember to put your cell phone on silent mode when you are in places that cell phones should not be heard.

- Remember to always be considerate while using your cell phone in public.

Cell Phone Class Discussion:

- Why should we lower our voices when talking on our cell phones in public? Have you heard people talking loudly on their cell phones? Does it bother you?

- What do you think of people who use foul language on their cell phones?

- Why should personal conversations not be heard by others? Should you lower your voice?

- Why should you not you take a call if someone is already in a conversation with you? Would you like someone to do the same to you?

- Why should you not text when someone is in a conversation with you?

- You aren't talking or recognizing the other person, just texting. Is that offensive to that person?

- Do you have some ideas of how you can remember to put your cell phone ringer on silent mode in theatres, places of worship, school and restaurants? Let's come up with some helpful ideas together.

- Why shouldn't you light up your phone screen in the theatre?

- Why shouldn't you talk on the phone while driving?

- Is it dangerous to use a cell phone while crossing the street?

- If you get a dropped call, whose fault is it? Why do you think it may have happened? Were there mountains around while you were driving? Could there not have been a cell tower? Should you let it upset you?

- Why is it rude to look up numbers or look on the Internet when you are in a conversation with someone? Being considerate should *always* be your Concern for another person talking with you in person.

- What difference does your ring tone make to others? Why? Is your cell phone ringer pleasant for others to hear?

- Can your cell phone become an actual life safer? Should you always carry it with you? What are some of the reasons you need it?

- Are you careful with the kind of language you use while leaving phone messages and texting? Words are extremely important and using the English language appropriately says a lot about your character.

- The use of cell phone, computers, iPods and iPads can become obsessive. Make sure that you have plenty of other interests during the day so that you are not always using these devices obsessively.

Cell Phone Scene Studies

Now that we have had a class discussion about the *how, when, why, and where* cell phones should and should not be used, let's have fun portraying the right and wrong kinds of cell phone and texting behaviors.

Exercise 1 -A Rude and Thoughtless Cell Phone Friend

It's almost time for spring break and Trisha and Brittany are planning a cruise with their parents to St. Thomas. Both girls are excited about their new adventure together and are out shopping for swim suits, shorts, and tops, etc. Their cruise is just two days away and they need to do all their new clothes shopping today. Brittany doesn't know how to choose her wardrobe very well and is depending on Trisha to help her choose the best colors and out fits for her.

We hear Tricia's cell phone Ring! Ring! Ring! Tricia answers excitely when she sees whose name is on her ID forgetting Brittany is standing there waiting for Tricia to help her with several swimming suits hanging on her arms.

Tricia: Hello. Oh, hi Graham! (giggling) How are you? Oh, nothing. Brittany and I are just out shopping. What's up? Sure I can be back home in Just an hour. Come on over, ok?

Brittany continues talking to Graham for the next fifteen minutes never acknowledging Brittany and the short time they have to buy new clothes. Finally Brittany gives Tricia a piece of her mind.

Brittany: Tricia, do you realize what time it is? Do you have any idea how rude you've been to me? I have been standing here waiting for you to end your conversation with Graham and you don't seem to know I'm alive. Forget about helping me with my clothes. I'll do it myself!

What do you think about Tricia? Is she a thoughtful, caring friend? Is she sensitive to Brittany? Is she rude to Brittany? What could Tricia do to be more considerate and thoughtful to Brittany? What could Tricia change about her phone conversation with Graham? Could Tricia benefit from knowing cell phone etiquette? Could she also learn about what it means to have a good friend?

Exercise2- A Polite and Considerate Cell Phone User

It's almost 3:00 pm and Myles is about to take his Wednesday afternoon Guitar lesson. As soon as his lesson is over he has to dash back to the gym and get ready for a basketball game tonight. His friend Josh keeps calling him on the way to his lesson bugging him about tonight's game.

Josh: Hey, Myles, I'm getting' nervous about tonight. What do you think? Do you think we'll be able to beat these guys? We're all countin' on you, man. You know you make the best long shots and you nail the basket better than any of us. We've got to beat these guys for real!.

Myles: Well, all I know is I'll do my best. I gotta go now, Josh. I'm getting ready to take my guitar lesson.

Josh: Ok, I'll call you later.

No sooner does Myles hang up that the phone rings again. It's Josh.

Myles wonders why does he keep calling me? Myles walks into Mr. Carlson's studio and greets his teacher.

Myles: Hi Mr. Carlson.

Mr. Carlson: Hi Myles. How's your music? Did you practice this week?

Myles: Yes sir, I did.

Mr. Carlson: Well, good. Let's turn to the section in your book and practice the first part of this piece about watching your rhythm.

Knowing that Josh will probably call again, Myles put his cell phone on silent mode before he walked into have his guitar lesson.

What is your impression of Josh? What is your impression of Myles? Did Myles think ahead about his lesson and teacher ahead of time? Thinking about your environment ahead of time is always a good idea when using good cell phone etiquette.

Now that we have discussed the wrong and right behaviors of using a cell phone in public, you can feel more confident in all of the above situations. You will know what to do or not to do. The most important thing for you to remember is to be considerate of others and by being aware of your environment you will make the right choices. Remember that people definitely notice cell phone behavior and it gives you a plus when you show that you are aware of being polite.

3. Different Cultures and Etiquette

The following study of different cultures and different etiquette is a fun study of the cultures and etiquette of these two countries. Read the material first and give some thought to teaching these two cultures if you have time. It is always a BIG hit with the students, especially learning to speak a few Japanese and Kenyan phrases.

It's Fun To Learn

Different Cultures
&
Different Etiquette

Around The World

Featuring....

Japan (Asia)

and

Kenya (Africa)

Did you know that every country around the world has a different culture and every country around the world has different types of etiquette?

In our country did you know that we have many, many different cultures? Can you name some of them? Where did they come from? *(e.g. Italian, Irish, Mexican, East Indian, African, Russian, French, Spanish, Swedish, Scottish and many more. It is wonderful to know that almost every culture in the world is represented here in America.)*

Have you ever wondered what does **culture** mean? *It means ways we have learned and shared together as a community. These certain ways become patterns that are socially accepted and patterns we practice.* For example, in America, our families gather around the dining room table at Thanksgiving. We usually have fall decorations or a horn of plenty in the center of the table. Why do we do this? Who cooks the turkey? Who usually carves it? These are patterns or traditions our country has shared for over three centuries. We come together to celebrate how our heavenly Father, who gave us our land and who protects us, who protected the pilgrims who traveled so far across the sea, and for our forefathers who founded our wonderful land. It is a warm and close time for us to look forward to each year.

Have you ever wondered what **Etiquette** means? *First of all it is a French word pronounced like ("eh-t-ket"). It is a code we go by that is expected within a society, social class or group. Mostly, etiquette means to be <u>considerate and polite</u>.* Can you think of some ways we use proper etiquette in our society?

Let's discuss the many different kinds of etiquette we practice in America.

- Table Manners

- Telephone/Cell Phone Etiquette

- Punctuality (being on time)

- Teacher/Student Etiquette

- Conversational Skills

- Introducing Someone To Someone Else

- Proper Attire

- Writing Letters & Thank You Notes

- Respect For Authority

- Friendship Etiquette

- Good Sportsmanship

- Being Tactful (means to be considerate; thoughtful)

- Manners Everywhere

- Being A Lady/Being A Gentleman

- Opening or Holding Doors for Others

- Offering A Seat To An Older Person

- Saying "Please", Thank You", You're Welcome", and Excuse Me"

These codes of behaviors are generally practiced in other cultures, but let's take a close look at the culture and etiquette codes of the beautiful Asian country of Japan. Has anyone ever visited Japan?

Japan

Who knows where Japan is located? Japan is located in the Far East of Asia. What is Japan's capitol? Tokyo.

Japan is known for its beautiful flower gardens and the Japanese are very hospitable people who love to entertain. They are the best at preparing lovely meals for their guests. In their culture it is appropriate to offer a gift to their guest when they arrive. Usually it is a memento worth keeping. If asked to someone's home in America, we might bring flowers, or if it is a friend's birthday, a card and a gift, but in Japan their custom is the exact opposite. They give a gift to their guest to honor them.

The Japanese are very formal. They are very comfortable being quiet and still. Have you ever noticed that a Japanese person doesn't smile very much? This is a cultural pattern. It does not mean that this person is sad. When a Japanese person smiles, they can light up a room!

They are a culture with an innate sense of what is right and what is wrong. If you offer a gesture of kindness, they will offer a gesture of kindness in return. Do you think we should practice some of their patterns in America? Why?

In America we may often bring a gift to say 'thank you' for having us to a special invitation to your home *(even if the host or hostess does not expect it.)* Both patterns define our different cultures. For example, the Japanese offer slip on shoes and socks to their guests when they arrive and the guests leave their other shoes outside of the front door. Why do you think they do this?

Have you ever visited a Japanese restaurant? What do they like to eat? What kind of drink do the Japanese like to serve? Yes, hot tea! What other cultures enjoy hot tea?*(China, England)* All of these are cultural patterns that are very hospitable and distinctively Japanese.

Some Basic Japanese Greetings:

Let's learn to say:

HELLO : Kon-nich-I-wa

GOODBYE: Sa-yo-na-ra

THANK YOU: Ari-got-toe

YOU'RE WELCOME: "lie lie"

    When a Japanese person hands you a business card it is with <u>both hands</u>. Isn't that interesting? It is given with a bow and is read very carefully. Is this much different from our culture? How do we hand another person our card? *We hand it with one hand and we do not bow.*

Let's ALL practice their way of giving a business card and add a bow the way they do.

A friend hands you their card and says:

    "Kon-nich ee-wa" (hello) to a new friend.

The friend says:

    "Ari-got-toe" (thank you).

Let's Take A Look At Japanese Etiquette:

Conversation:

*Bow when greeting someone

*Do not speak loudly

*Do not blow their nose in public

*Do not display emotion

*The Japanese have difficulty saying no

*Do not put their hands in their pockets

In Business:

*Bow in greeting

*Exchange business cards

*Do not slouch

Females should avoid heels

Moments of silence are normal

Do not interrupt. Listen carefully

Dining:

*It is acceptable to

make noise while eating

*Rice left in your bowl

*Try any foods offered

*All courses are served at once

*Cross legs at the ankle indicates the desire for seconds

Leisure:

*Remove shoes before Entering homes

*Wear surgical masks when they have a cold

Restaurants:

*Men sit cross-legged and women sit with their legs to the side

Culture and etiquette are two very important words, because by understanding them and practicing them, we will have a wider knowledge of why people from different countries are different from each other. Discovering other cultures and their ways of doing things makes our world so very interesting.

Let's Pretend We Are In Japan!

Jenny and Paul are on a mission trip here in Tokyo, Japan, this country's capitol. They have made friends with Su Lyn and her brother, Keioko and they have had a lot of fun together. Su Lyn and Keioko have invited Jenny and Paul over for dinner, and Paul and Jenny are real excited to see what it's like to have dinner in a Japanese home.

Who would like to portray Su Lynn and Keioko?

We also need a boy and girl to portray Jenny and Paul.

(Jenny and Paul knock on the door of their new Japanese friend's door.

Su Lynn opens the door

Su Lynn: Wataschi no ie wo kangei suru, Jenny & Paul. *(meaning welcome to my home in Japanese.)*

(She bows to them and Jenny and Paul respectfully bow in return.)

Keioko: Japanese custom is to take off shoes before entering house.

(Jenny and Paul take off their shoes and Su Lynn offers them sandals and socks to wear inside)

Su Lyn offers their new friends from America a little gift to thank them for coming to visit them and gestures for them to sit and relax at their table with pillows on the floor.

Keioko: Come sit down and relax. Would you like a cup of hot tea?

Jenny: Yes. I love hot tea! It's cold outside. It will warm us up!

Su Lyn: Japanese eat lots of rice. Do Americans like rice?

Paul: Yes, we like rice, but I don't think we eat as much of it as you do!! (All of them laugh.)

Su Lyn: We eat rice with chop sticks. You like chop sticks?

Jenny: Oh, yes. Chop sticks are fun!

Let's skip forward to the end of the evening:

Jenny says: We had a wonderful time learning about your customs and seeing how the Japanese live, didn't we Paul?"

Paul: Oh, yes! I wish we had cushions to sit on at home like these *(as he fluffs them)* and I want to get some chop sticks!!

Jenny and Paul graciously bow to them as they say Ari-gato

(meaning "thank you" in Japanese).

Su Lyn and Kieoko say: Lie lie" *(you're welcome in Japanese)* We had much fun having you two as our guests. You must come and visit us many times!"

Jenny and Paul say together: We promise to. Sa-yo-na-ra.

Su Lyn and Kieoko say together: Sa-yo-na-ra

Kenya

Who can tell me the location of Kenya, Africa? Kenya is located in Eastern Africa, bordering the Indian Ocean, between Jamalia and Tanzania. Who knows its capitol? The capitol is Nairobi. Kenya is made up 40 or more ethnic groups. Each has its own dialect. Isn't that interesting?

What are the Kenyan People like? Kenyans are friendly and hospitable people. Greetings are an important part of social and business interaction.

What Language Do The Kenyan's Speak? The Kenyan's speak English and Swahili. They also speak their own dialects which are indigenous or native to the region where they life.

Family is very important to Kenyans. They usually have a large and extended family and they treat their elderly with respect and honor.

What Do Kenyan Kids Like To Eat and Drink? They like to eat chicken, rice, goat, and tilapia. They enjoy fresh fruit and veggies. *(All good stuff!)* They like to drink tea with milk and sugar served with breakfast and at tea time in the late afternoon. Where do you think they originally got this pattern? From the British!

Kenya's Art and Artifacts: Kenya's art is known and admired around the world for its beautifully carved wood sculpture made with local materials and sold abroad. Look for museums which display Kenya's art and history. Kenya is also recognized for its hand woven baskets, jewelry, musical instruments, figurines and African sarongs.

Music and Dance: Traditional music and dance are an integral part of Kenyan social and religious lives. These two arts play an important part of Kenya culture and tradition.

Kenya's Most Popular Sport: Kenya's most popular sport is Soccer, however their long distance runners have gained international recognition. Athletes around the world look up to Kenyan legends.

Kenyan Greetings

Let's learn to say these greetings and phrases In Kenyan Language:

Hello: *Jambo*

Goodbye: *Kwaheri*

Thank You: *Asante*

What is your name?   *Jina lako nani?*

Let's Play

"Get To Know You Game"

Every one find a partner. Pretend you have never met.

No. 1 person starts by saying **Jambo** (hello) in Swahili

No .2 person also says **Jambo.** (Both smile at each other)

No. 1 person asks: **Jina lako nani?** (what is your name?)

No. 2 person answers his or her name in English.

No. 2 also asks: **Jina lako nani?**

No. 1 answers his or her name.

Let's Learn About Kenyan Etiquette:

Conversation: The hand shake is a common greeting

They engage in small talk

Kenyans do not like to say no or yes

They are humorous people

They love to laugh

Business: They use their right hand to receive gifts

They are prepared in business.

Meetings are usually long.

Kenyans prefer to make group decisions

Dining: Eating is taken very seriously

Eating is usually done in silence

Lunch is the most important meal of the day

The evening meal tends to be light

Traditional foods are eaten without utensils using the left hand

Here is A Fun Game Kenyan Children Love To Play Called

Mbube Mbube

(pronounced "Mboo-bay Mboo-bay)

In this game the children help the lion (mbube) to locate and capture an impala (a deer-like animal with antlers. The children begin game standing in a circle. Two blindfolded players start the game. One player is the **Lion** and the other is the **Impala.**

- First, both the lion and impala are spun around.

- Next, the other children call out to the lion, *"mbube, mbube!!"*

- As the impala gets closer to the lion, the children shout *"mbube, mbube"* louder and louder!!!

- If the lion is far away, the children's voices get softer and softer.

- If the lion fails to catch the impala in one minute, a new lion is chosen and if the new lion catches the impala, then the games continues.

Learning about new cultures and their social behaviors and etiquette is very interesting, isn't it? Today we have learned quite a lot about two other cultures, Japan and Kenya, Africa which are located in two different areas of the world. Would you say that these two cultures are different from one another? Are they different from ours in America? In what ways do you think they may be the same? Do you think that we should practice some of the cultural patterns and etiquette of Japan and those of Kenya, Africa? Let's have a class discussion.

Best Wishes from the Author

Now we've come to the close of our study with **God's Best Is Me**, but it is a new beginning for you! You have learned much more about yourself, the world around you, and what God expects of you!

Creating these studies in **God's Best Is Me** was a great joy for me. Each topic was carefully chosen to inspire you to apply what you have learned to be a true "Quality Person".

Apostle Paul tells us in Romans 12:1-2:

"Do not conform any longer to the pattern of this world,

but be transformed by the renewing of your mind.

Then you will be able to test and approve what God's will is…

His good and pleasing, perfect will."

Never forget that the way you live, the way you think, the words you say, and the way you treat others has a great influence on our world. I have confidence that YOU are going to make a positive difference for us all!

Wherever you may go in life, remember these beautiful thoughts written by our mentor, the Apostle Paul, and keep them close to your heart:

> *"Whatsoever things are true*
> *Whatsoever things are honest*
> *Whatsoever things are pure*
> *Whatsoever things are lovely*
> *Think on these things.*
> *And above all these things,*
> *Let the Peace of God rule in your hearts."*
> **Philippians 4:8**

And always remember to be children of light. Walk in the footsteps of the Apostle Paul and boldly tell everyone about Jesus Christ.

Suggestions for Teaching God's Best Is Me

The following settings suggest how *God's Best Is Me* may be studied:

- In a group setting of children ages 6 to 8, 9 to 12 and 13 to 17.

- It may also be taught privately in the home, with a group or individually.

- Have an instructor oversee all of these studies and interaction, especially in a group class.

There is a companion Teacher's Guide to this book also available on-line or at SouthernGracePlaceUSA.com

- Each student will need to include her or his Bible, along with the *God's Best Is Me* Student Manual each week.

- Please feel free to ☎ call Dr. Jeanne Sheffield at (202) 716-6444 or email ✉ DrJeanne@SouthernGracePlaceUSA.com to discuss questions you may have in regards to *God's Best Is Me* including craft ideas or special projects.

- Dr. Jeanne Sheffield is available to give *God's Best Is Me* presentations or workshops for your church, school, home school, or civic organization. You may reach her at ☎ (202) 716-6444 or by email at ✉ Dr.Jeanne@ SouthernGracePlaceUSA.com

God's Best Is Me

Songs of
Praise

To Live and Love By!

The *God's Best Is Me* Song Book & CD accompaniment can be ordered by:

Telephone: 202-716-6444

Email: DrJeanne@SouthernGracePlaceUSA.com

Copyright © 2012, Dr. Jeanne Sheffield.

All rights reserved.

God Brings Out The Very Best In Me

Words & Music By Jeanne Sheffield

I'm learning how to love
Learning how to share
I'm learning how to give
Learning more to care

Opening my heart
Offering my hand
To my fellow man

I'm watching what I say
I'm watching what I do
Making sure I pray
Not just for me, but you

And every single day
In every single way
I can see the change in me
God brings out the very best in me
Yes, God brings out the very best in me

Every day in every way
God brings out the best in me

Repeat Song
Offering my hand
To help my fellow man

I Walk in Grace

Words & Music by Jeanne Sheffield

I walk in grace

I walk in love
I walk in grace
Sent from heaven above

I walk in grace

I walk in love
I walk in grace
God's loving grace

And I am growing stronger
I am growing tall
Following the footsteps
Of the great Apostle Paul

I walk in grace

I walk with Christ
I walk in grace
I am proud He's my life

And I am growing stronger
I am growing tall
Following the footsteps
Of the great Apostle Paul

Walking in grace
Walking in grace
Here I am a child of God
Walking in grace

The Fruit of the Spirit

Author Unknown

(VBS song to the tune of "If You're Happy and You Know It)

Oh the fruit of the spirit's not an apple
Oh the fruit of the spirit's not an apple

If you want to be an apple

Then you might as well hear it

You can't be a fruit of the spirit

'Cause they are Love, Joy, Peace, Patience, Kindness, Goodness, Faithfulness, Gentleness, and Self-Control!

Oh the fruit of the spirit's not a grape
Oh the fruit of the spirit's not a grape

If you want to be a grape

Then you might as well hear it

You can't be a fruit of the spirit

'Cause they are Love, Joy, Peace, Patience, Kindness, Goodness, Faithfulness, Gentleness, and Self-Control!

Oh the fruit of the spirit's not a lemon
Oh the fruit of the spirit's not a lemon

If you want to be a lemon

Then you might as well hear it

You can't be a fruit of the spirit

'Cause they are Love, Joy, Peace, Patience, Kindness, Goodness, Faithfulness, Gentleness, and Self-Control!

Oh the fruit of the spirit's not a banana
Oh the fruit of the spirit's not a banana

If you want to be a banana

Then you might as well hear it

You can't be a fruit of the spirit

'Cause they are Love, Joy, Peace, Patience, Kindness, Goodness, Faithfulness, Gentleness, and Self-Control!

Love Stretches My Heart

Words & Music by Jeanne Sheffield

Love stretches my heart
And makes me big inside!

Love stretches my heart
And makes me big inside!

God's love stretches
God's love stretches
God's love stretches
When you open your heart wide (end here)
Repeat:

And I am God's own vessel
Overflowing with His love
Yes, I am God's own vessel
These two arms were made to hug

Yes I am God's vessel
My purpose here is clear
I'll show the world that Jesus lives
He lives inside of here

Back to top:

Attitude Says A Lot

Words & Music by Jeanne Sheffield

Verse 1

Attitude, Attitude

Is how you wake up and greet the day, hey!

Verse 2

Attitude, Attitude

Shows up in every little word you say!

Chorus

Attitude can be positive (speak)

It can be quite negative, too

Attitude is a choice you make (sing)

It all depends on you! (speak)

Verse 3

Attitude, Attitude

Makes people wanna stop and notice you!

(who me? Yes!)

Repeat Chorus

Verse 5

Attitude, Attitude

Says you're happy with the way you are!

Verse 6

Attitude, Attitude

Says you can wish on a falling star! Ah….(sigh)!

Repeat Chorus

End

Attitude is in your gratitude

So let's be thankful to God each day (yeah!)

Attitude says a lot! (speak)

Always Be Kind, Always Be Gentle

Words & Music by Jeanne Sheffield

Verse 1

Always be kind, always be gentle
Give from your heart, show that you care

Verse 2

Always be kind when someone needs you
Be a good friend and willing to share
(Be loyal and true) 2nd time 2xx

Chorus 1

Your smile can turn
A cloudy day to sunshine
Why don't you try it when someone's lost their way

Verse 3

Always be kind, always be gentle
Put someone first
Before yourself

Chorus 2

Always be kind (repeat 2x)
And understanding God is watching
Making sure you are following his commands
(Repeat top of song)

End:

Always be kind and gentle to everyone
To everyone

A Real Good Friend

Words & Music by Jeanne Sheffield

Are you a real good friend?
Can I count on you?
Are you a real good friend?
Loyal, honest and true?

Chorus:
'Cause if you
I have found a treasure
yeah, if you are
I'm the lucky one

'Cause if you are
We;ll be close friends forever
Sharin' the good times
Carein' through the hard times
Lovin' life because
We've found a friend

Are you a real good friend?
One to tell my secrets to?
Are you a real good friend?
Make me smile when I'm blue?

Repeat Chorus:

End: I think I've found a real good friend

Sweet Joy

Words & Music by Jeanne Sheffield

I've got joy overflowing
I've got joy down to my soul
I've got joy and it's growing
Gonna get me more and more

I've got joy in the mornin'
When I meet the risin' sun
So much joy keeps on growin'
For my Father and His Son

Sweet Joy
Sweet Joy
Nothin' can compete
With this happiness so sweet

Sweet Joy
Sweet Joy
Livin' in the presence of sweet joy

I've got joy overflowin'
Blessin' every one I meet
Joy keeps pourin' down from heaven
And it's absolutely free

Sweet Joy
Sweet Joy
Nothin' can compare
To the joy you'll want to share

Sweet Joy
Sweet Joy
Livin' in the presence of sweet joy
Livin' in the presence of sweet joy

Peace, Be Still

Words & Music by Jeanne Sheffield

Sometimes when you're worried
Sometimes when you're scared
Sometimes when you're frightened
And nobody's there

Sometimes when you're lonely
Sometimes when you cry
Sometimes when you lose
The dearest person in your life

Give it up to Jesus
He'll calm you in the storm
Give it up to Jesus
He'll keep you safe and warm

Peace, Be still
Peace, Be still

Sometimes when you're hurried
Sometimes when you fall
Sometimes when you live alone
And there's no one you can call

Sometimes when your heart breaks
Sometimes when love ends
Sometimes when your future
Is lookin' mighty dim

Give it up to Jesus
He'll calm you in the storm
Give it up to Jesus
He'll keep you safe and warm

Peace, Be still, Peace, Be still

Be a Package of Goodness

Words & Music by Jeanne Sheffield

Verse1:
Be a package of goodness
To everyone you know
Be a package of goodness
No matter where you go

Verse 2:
Be a package of goodness
Wrap yourself in one big bow
And soon you'll find
Your love will over flow

Over flow
Over flow
Over flow
Over flow

Be a package of goodness
And let your love
Start to over flow!

Verse:
Be a package of goodness
Sing and praise the living Word
Be a package of goodness
So many haven't heard

Verse 4:
Be a package of goodness
Why not go the extra mile?
And soon you'll find your love
Will over flow

Over flow
Over flow
Over flow
Over flow

Be a package of goodness
God's kind of goodness
Be a package of goodness
And watch your love over flow!

The Circle of Love

Words & Music by Jeanne Sheffield and Celia McRee

The circle of love is an endless connection

A chain of affection for all
The circle of love is a world full of laughter
Where nobody cries if they fall, even if they're small

The circle of love has no start and no finish
And everyone in it is a friend
The circle of love doesn't have any limit
So why don't you come right on in
To the circle of love, the circle of love, the circle of love

The circle of love is like finding a rainbow
Where all of your dreams do come true
The circle of love is like playing in sunshine
Where blue skies are always in view, Shining down on you

The circle of love is like being a princess
A knight dressed in armor, a king
Anything you can dream
So come on and let's sing (la, la's…)

The circle of love has its arms all around you
Love around you're in the middle of joy
The circle of love is so happy it found you
Everyone, be it girl, be it boy
Doesn't matter, it's great to be here
Here in the circle of love (Repeat la la's…)

The circle of love keeps on going forever
And doesn't care whether you're tall or small
Young or old, king or queen
You can be anything

Be all your dreams
Be in the circle of love (repeat)

Come Take My Hand

Words & Music by Jeanne Sheffield

Come take my hand

Let's go down by the river
Come take my hand and let's meet the Lord
I understand He loves all of His children
He loves to sing and He laughs when we play

Come take my hand

Let's go down by the river
We'll be surprised at the children we see
All of them loving His glorious presence
Wanting a kiss on the cheek

Come and go down to the river with me
We'll meet the Master who sets the world free!

Come take my hand
Children of God
Let's all join hands
Let's praise the Lord
(Repeat)

Let's go and meet Him (solo)
I heard he tells stories
Filling our hearts with such wonderful Joy!
Don't be surprised if He already knows us (solo)
He watches over whenever we sleep

Come and go down to the river with me
We'll meet the Master who sets the world free!
Let's all join hands
Children of God
Let's go and praise the Lord
Come take my hand
What a new exciting experience
This will be!

Patient Spirit

Words & Music by Jeanne Sheffield

Verse 1:
Please God, give me Your patience
When I want things to go my way
Please God, give me Your patience

Chorus:
And help me to be gentle
Kind and considerate
Being calm and so together
Give me Your patient Spirit

Please God, give me your Spirit
Show me what You would do
Please God, give me your Spirit
I always want to please you

Chorus:
I help me to be gentle
Kind and considerate
Being calm and so together
Give me your patient Spirit

End:
When I start my day
Watch the words I say
Lord, I want to be patient like you